BBC MUSIC GUIDES

———

SCHUMANN SONGS

BBC MUSIC GUIDES

Schumann Songs

ASTRA DESMOND

UNIVERSITY OF WASHINGTON PRESS

SEATTLE

First published 1972 by the British Broadcasting Corporation
Copyright © Astra Desmond 1972
University of Washington Press edition first published 1972
Library of Congress Catalog Card Number 74-39503
ISBN 0-295-95200-8
Printed in England

Contents

Introduction

For a full understanding of Robert Schumann's songs it is desirable to know something of his life and antecedents. His father, August Schumann, was a remarkable man. Though not a musician, he had strong artistic and literary leanings. Through many vicissitudes he had succeeded in establishing himself in a bookshop in Zwickau, Saxony, where Robert was born on 8 June 1810. From his father Robert inherited his creative urge and a determination to achieve his objective, which was to be demonstrated in his struggle to obtain his wife in face of strong parental opposition. His mother, Johanna Schumann, was of an emotional and sentimental nature, and it is perhaps from her that Robert inherited the instability of temperament that was later to prove fatal to him.

From the age of seven he studied the piano, showing a great aptitude for the instrument. In every way his father encouraged him and gave him opportunities for hearing good performers and making music. On the literary side, he gave him access to books from his shop, thereby giving him a wider culture than he would have had if he had concentrated only on music. He acquired a wide knowledge of classical and modern literature, especially the works of Jean Paul Richter, who became his idol. Richter's works helped to increase his extreme sensibility. They certainly were responsible for encouraging both his natural leaning to sentimentality and his idea of a dual personality. His division of his own personality into Eusebius the dreamer and Florestan the impulsive one was clearly modelled upon Vult and Walt of Richter's novel *Die Flegeljahre*.

The death of August Schumann in 1826, coming soon after the death of his nineteen-year-old sister Emilie, who drowned herself, was a severe shock to the boy at a very impressionable age, from which he never quite recovered and which increased the strain of melancholy from which he suffered periodically throughout his life. His mother sent him to the University of Leipzig to study law.

Living in Leipzig at the time were the famous piano-teacher Friedrich Wieck and his little daughter Clara, then only nine years old, but already a brilliant pianist. Neglecting his law studies, he began taking lessons from Wieck and later entered the Wieck household as a resident pupil. Soon a fast friendship grew up between the young man and the little girl.

In 1832, while the Wiecks were away on tour, he invented a contraption for improving the technique of his left hand. Instead of improving it, however, it caused such injury to his hand that he had to give up all ideas of a career as a concert pianist. He accordingly turned his energies to becoming a composer.

As well as his father and sister, two brothers, a favourite sister-in-law and a bosom friend all died within the space of a few years, followed soon after by his mother. Meanwhile Clara Wieck was growing up and at sixteen she was, after her successful concert tours, remarkably mature for her years. Schumann began to realise how much her sympathy and her understanding of his difficult nature meant to him. Her childish hero-worship had ripened into love and the young people became secretly engaged. Wieck, suspecting what was happening, had, quite understandably, other ideas for his talented daughter than marriage with an, as yet, obscure and impecunious young composer. So he promptly sent Clara away and forbade any communication between the two. However, when Clara reached eighteen they became openly engaged. Wieck was quite irreconcilable, so in 1839 when Clara was twenty they resorted to the courts to get permission to marry without her father's consent.

During the years 1827–8 Schumann had written eleven songs dedicated to his three sisters-in-law. Two, hitherto attributed to a non-existent poet Ekert, 'Sehnsucht' and 'Hirtenknabe', were settings of Schumann's own texts; one was after Byron, 'Die Weinende'; Goethe's 'Der Fischer'; five by Justinus Kerner, 'Kurzes Erwachen', 'Gesanges Erwachen', 'An Anna I & II', and 'Im Herbste'; and 'Erinnerung' and 'Klage' by Jacobi. These he sent to Gottlob Wiedebein, the musical director at Brunswick, himself a composer of songs. Wiedebein replied: 'They have many shortcomings, but Nature has been very kind to you; make the most of your talent and the world will not withhold its approbation.' The songs were not published at the time but Schumann used 'An Anna II' in the piano sonata Op. 11; 'Im Herbste' in Op. 22, and 'Hirtenknabe' in the Intermezzo, Op. 4, no. 4. Brahms published these three in the Collected Edition of 1893; 'Der Fischer' appeared in the *Zeitschrift für Musik* in 1933; 'Klage' was never finished and the remainder were published by Karl Geiringer in 1933. Schumann wrote no more songs until 1840.

The Wonderful Year Begins:
the Heine Liederkreis and Myrthen

By the beginning of 1840 Schumann had reached the summit of his powers as a composer for the piano. But now the possibility of marriage and the assurance of Clara's love needed something more to express the excitement that was bubbling up inside him and there burst from him a spate of songs so that within the space of a year he produced about 140, among them his greatest masterpieces. He wrote to Clara at this time, 'Oh Clara, what bliss to write songs! Too long I have refrained from doing so' and 'I should like to sing myself to death like a nightingale'.

His response to poetry was subjective and his best songs were those which touched a personal chord in himself. Musically, he was chiefly influenced by Beethoven, especially by his cycle *An die ferne Geliebte*, and by Schubert, whom he loved and often quoted. (It is said that when Schubert died in 1828 Schumann sobbed all night.) He was essentially a romantic of the nineteenth century, a mystic, and completely in tune with the romantic poets of his own generation, drawn like them to the dream-world of nature, of birds and flowers as symbols of love. The poet whose poetry corresponded most closely to his own experience was Heine and to him he turned for over forty of his finest songs. What Goethe was to Schubert, Heine was to Schumann.

But the real mainspring of his inspiration was undoubtedly Clara. In his monumental work on the songs,[1] Eric Sams has worked out, with great ingenuity, the proof of this in the themes and codes to be found in the music; a subject far too large and complex for a slight volume like this. Readers interested in the subject are referred to Mr Sams' writings, and I should like to pay tribute to the valuable information his book has given me, and for his chronology of the dates of composition, which for the most part I have followed.

The earliest song of 1840 was a setting of Feste's song from a translation of Shakespeare's *Twelfth Night*, 'Schlusslied des Narren'. It was probably inspired by the composer's admiration for his friend Mendelssohn's music for *A Midsummer Night's Dream*. It is

[1] *The Songs of Robert Schumann* (London, 1969).

9

quite attractive but was not published till much later in Op. 125. The second and fourth verses are omitted. His next setting was of Heine's 'Belsazar', though he did not publish it until 1847 as Op. 57. It tells the well-known biblical story of the King of Babylon and the writing on the wall. It opens with the theme:

Ex. 1

Im Anfange nicht zu schnell, nach und nach rascher

(Not too fast at first, but gradually increasing the pace)

which recurs at intervals. It is broken by quaver figures on the piano at 'da flackert's' as flashes from the palace torches light up the scene; then there is a martial theme for the assembled courtiers and a noisy clatter of staccato chords for their drunken applause. The music quietens for a while as the king drinks from the golden cup, stolen from the Temple. Uneasy octaves suggest the fear of the guests as he blasphemes. The drama gets a little weak at the moment of the appearance of the writing and it concludes with a recitative passage leaving the drama to the skill of the singer. It can be very effective if well sung.

It was Schumann's habit to concentrate on one poet at a time and many of his songs are collected in cyclic form. From Heine's *Buch der Lieder* he selected nine lyrics for a Heine *Liederkreis* and dedicated them to Pauline Viardot, then at the height of her career. They form Op. 24 and begin with 'Morgens steh' ich auf und frage' (Every morning I wonder 'will she come today?' Every evening I lie down sleepless). This little song was evidently inspired by Clara's absence. It has a charming tripping piano part in contrary motion, Schumann's characteristic syncopation and the turn, typical of his early songs but rarely used in later songs. In 'Es treibt mich hin' the lover waits impatiently for the beloved's return: 'the hours are so slow, they can surely never have been in love!' An outburst of impatience carries the voice over a wide range. There is a choice of alternative notes in the voice-part, such as occurs in other songs. Schumann is perhaps thinking of his own precept: 'You should early come to understand the compass of the human voice.' So when the melody goes extra high or low he is considerate enough to give alternative notes. Generally speaking it seems desirable, if possible, to follow the melody of the piano accompaniment. The postlude carries on the feeling of impatience with much syncopation. Now comes one of the most beautiful songs in the cycle, no. 3, 'Ich wandelte unter den Bäumen'. The poet is alone in the woods and the old dreams creep into his heart. Here a lovely phrase in triplet crotchets interrupts the four–four time. He asks the birds, who taught them his secret? The key changes to G major and the treble clef high on the stave as the birds answer that a maiden taught it to them. Back in B major he rebukes them for telling him. Schumann has the psychological insight to enter into the poet's obstinate refusal to be comforted, he will 'trust no one'.

Already in his short life Schumann had become familiar with death, and thoughts of death found an immediate response in him for the curious poem 'Lieb' Liebchen leg's Händchen' in a very original and remarkable setting. The voice enters unaccompanied and proceeds with only short syncopated chords on the piano. The poet bids his love feel the beat of his heart. He likens it to the hammer strokes of a carpenter making his coffin. A C flat in the bass on the piano gives a sinister feeling to the harmless word 'Zimmermann' (carpenter) and then an original touch of dread is given by the breaking-off of the voice as if not daring to say the word 'coffin'. The piano finishes the phrase, then the voice plucks up courage to pronounce the word 'Totensarg'.

Ex. 2

The song is in strophic form and the same device perfectly fits the words of the second verse. In this song Schumann has wonderfully reproduced the neurotic quality of the verses.

No. 5, 'Schöne Wiege meiner Leiden', finds Heine in a nostalgic mood. As a young man he had been sent to live with rich relations in Hamburg; he was very unhappy there and is reputed to have been snubbed by his uncle when he fell in love with his pretty cousin. Perhaps the composer's own rebuff by Clara's father attracted him to the poem in spite of its length. The idea of the cradle obviously inspired the rocking movement in the piano part. For the first time in this cycle the voice breaks away from the piano melody and is independent. Heine is in his most self-pitying mood and Schumann follows all his grievances very sympathetically, with a passionate outburst of harsh chords at 'you drive me away' and syncopated scale passages at 'Madness is in my heart'. A return to the opening lines is followed by more repetitions of 'Lebewohl' and a postlude concludes the song in a chain almost entirely consisting of diminished sevenths. This song is followed by 'Warte, warte, wilder Schiffsmann', a bravura piece for the pianist, in which the poet bids farewell to Europe and his love to staccato octave passages on the piano. Two points worth noticing are the syncopation at 'schaudert mein Blut zu seh'n', suggesting the beloved's recoil at the sight of his blood; and the alternative notes at 'lange Jahre' presumably put in to help a voice that finds the lower notes impracticable. These are preferable as the syncopation carries out the idea of 'long years' better than the high ones on the beat. No. 7, 'Berg und Burgen schau'n herunter', has four verses in strophic form with only slight changes to fit the words. A waving figure on the piano suggests the boat drifting on the lapping water. The poet reflects that under the golden radiance of the water lie death and night. The river is the image of the beloved, she too had a gentle smile. There is no indication in the music of the implication of treachery that the words bear. In verse three the score has 'bringt' as in the earliest edition of the poem, but Heine's later revision to 'birgt' makes better sense. No. 8, 'Anfangs wollt' ich fast verzagen', has only eleven bars of music. 'At first I was in despair and thought I could never bear it; yet I have borne it, never ask me: how?' The piano part is all in the bass clef, sturdy crotchet chords of endurance, with no

nuance except at the end in a hushed repetition of 'nicht wie?'
The last song is the envoi for the next work, *Myrthen*, which was
to be a wedding present for Clara, 'Mit Myrthen und Rosen'.
'With myrtles and roses and rich gilt I would adorn this book as
a shrine wherein to bury my songs. When the book comes into
your dear hands the pale letters will glow and whisper a sigh of
love.' This is the first song to have Schumann's favourite direction
'innig'. How is it to be translated? The dictionary has 'intimate',
'close', 'fond', 'fervent', 'devout', 'heartfelt', 'cordial' and 'tender'.
As used by Schumann, it has something of all these meanings and
yet something more in his best songs. This song, with its long
flowing melody and warm enthusiasm, has great variety of expression and well reflects the composer's feeling at this time.

The book promised was duly produced and presented. The
publisher was instructed to have the volume as beautifully bound
and tastefully designed as possible. To Clara he wrote: 'As I wrote,
I wept for joy.' The volume is called *Myrthen*, Op. 25, and contains
many of Schumann's best-known and loved songs. It is not
strictly a cycle, but the twenty-six songs are generally in key
relation to each other and have some personal angle. They are by
various poets.

If 'Mit Myrthen und Rosen' was the envoi, then the first song
'Widmung' is the dedication. The words are by Friedrich Rückert,
the first of many by him to be set by Schumann. It is a perfect
song of love and gratitude to the woman who has been the
inspiration of his music and the solace of his heart. This song also
is marked 'innig', and whoever can feel the essence of this beautiful
song knows what is meant by *Innigkeit*. The warm uprush of
arpeggios at the beginning have a lovely change of key from A flat
to E major at 'Du bist die Ruh' and crotchet chords in triplets over
a sustained bass, as the lover expresses his reverence for the woman
who has revealed him to himself and lifted him above his highest
hopes. The key then returns to A flat major in a reprise of the first
lines and the postlude ends with a quotation from Schubert's
'Ave Maria'. The second song, 'Freisinn', by Goethe, is an
example of how Schumann sometimes took a poem literally,
without regard to any possible deeper significance the poet may
have had in mind; Goethe's free-thought probably meant a great
deal more to him than this fresh little song of youthful independ-

ence. A well-loved masterpiece is the third song, 'Der Nussbaum', by a great friend Julius Mosen. Swaying arpeggios on the piano and a melody, shared alternately with the voice, create a drowsy atmosphere for the dreaming girl. Delicate word-painting at 'flüstern', a lovely phrase at 'wusste selber nicht was', a vocal line that drops as she sinks into a dreamy sleep, all combine to make an exquisite tone-picture. As often, Schumann does not scruple to alter a poem for his musical convenience. He has substituted the more expressive 'Blätter' for the original 'Äste' and ignored the verse form of 'leise' and its rhyming 'Weise'. But one cannot cavil at such literary liberties when the result is so lovely a song.

A German version of Robert Burns's lyrics by Wilhelm Gerhard provided texts for nine songs, eight in Op. 25 and one in Op. 27. The first of these is 'Jemand' (For the sake o' somebody). A delicate and wistful setting begins in E minor as the girl bewails her separation from the loved one in a simple tune over detached staccato chords on the piano. The key changes to the major as she prays to the heavenly powers to protect him. Ex. 3 shows the poignant harmony Schumann achieves so effectively:

Ex. 3

die ihr der Lie – be hold,

At her passionate outburst of 'O Wonne! dem Jemand' the accompaniment becomes richer, then the 2/4 time changes to 6/8 at 'What wad I not for Somebody'. In 'Die Hochländer Witwe' (The Highland widow's lament) the German version has quite successfully reproduced the original rhythm and Schumann keeps the pulse going with a strong driving accompaniment. The minor key changes for a moment to the major as the widow thinks of joys of the past, then back in the minor there is a build-up to the climax at 'O weh, o weh!' No. 13, 'Hochländers Abschied' (My heart's in the Highlands) is another exile's song but without bitterness or self-pity; again poet and composer show a nice feeling for Burns's original metre. No. 14, 'Hochländisches Wiegenlied' (Hee Balou) is set strophically to a rocking movement in both voice and piano and is an exquisite lullaby worthy to stand beside Brahms's. No. 19 is 'Hauptmanns Weib' (The Captain's Lady). The German text builds the lady up into a sort of Amazon with steel armour, helm and sword, not at all the lady of Burns's text. However, the result is a vigorous and attractive song with fine drum-rolls and marching rhythm. The next, 'Weit, weit' (The bonnie lad that's far awa'), is a plaintive strophic song. Two verses are omitted from the original poem, one by the translator and one by the composer; it would hardly have done to include 'my bonnie babie will be born' in a bridal gift. 'Niemand' (I hae a wife o' my ain) is marked 'Seitenstück zu "Jemand"' quite wrongly, as in Burns the two poems have no connection. This is a married man boasting of his independence, summed up in 'If naebody troubles me, I'll trouble naebody'. This cheerful song is set in quavers, which change to two descending crotchets at each mention of 'Niemand', holding up the rhythm in an attractive way. The last of the Burns songs is 'Im Westen' (Out over the Forth). Without pre- or postlude the song is very short with an effective change of rhythm and accompaniment when, after scorning three points of the compass, the poet praises the West where all his loved ones are.

To return to the earlier songs of Op. 25, there are two from Goethe's *Schenkenbuch im Divan*; first, 'Sitz' ich allein', in which the poet asks for nothing better than to be left alone with his thoughts and a glass of wine. The rather solid 2/4 time changes to 6/8 in C major at the happy thought that no one can bother him and interrupt his thoughts. The other song is 'Setze mir nicht', a complete contrast. After a few bars of clumping octaves the voice breaks in petulantly, 'Don't bang the jug down so clumsily under my nose, you lout', then the A minor key changes to the major and more flowing music as the poet catches sight of a charming boy standing by the window; he calls to him and bids him serve his wine. The postlude dances away in contented leaps. It is a pleasant irony that at the time Schumann was writing these songs, Wieck was making his last throw to avert the marriage by accusing him of drunkenness.

A loved and famous song is 'Die Lotosblume' from Heine's *Lyrisches Intermezzo*. Heine's symbolism is here at its most imaginative. Slow crotchet chords convey the emotion over a slow sustained bass typifying the calm lake on which the flower is floating. There is an odd lapse of Schumann's usual taste in word setting, where he allows a silent gap in the voice for three whole beats between the verb 'ängstigt' and its reflexive 'sich' so that the singer must hold fast to the sense, through the rests, so as to avoid landing 'sich' with a bump on the first beat of the next bar. The lotus flower, tortured by the sun's hot light, awaits the coming of the moon. There is a magical plunge from C major into A flat major at the mention of the moon, her lover. Only for him will she unveil her face; here there is a lovely curving phrase for the lift of her head. Then the music increases in intensity as she gazes and trembles with love and the pain of love.

Two songs by Goethe follow, 'Talismane', a fine declamatory song praising God as Lord of the world. An interesting passage which recalls Handel's straying sheep in *Messiah* occurs at 'Mich verwirren will das Irren'. The second song, 'Lied der Suleika', though attributed to Goethe, is more probably by Marianne von Willemer. It is a pure love-song of unalloyed happiness. It opens with an arpeggio quoted from 'Widmung'. In this song we feel for a moment that all the composer's own fears and frustrations are laid aside. Two songs by Rückert are 'Lied der Braut', nos. 1 and 2. These were written, he told Clara, for her to sing for herself. These poems evidently moved him, very ready as he was to explore the mind of a young bride-to-be, and they are set with much tenderness. The first is a passionate one, as the bride reassures her mother of her continuing love; the second is in a solemn vein, telling her mother not to fear the outcome of her marriage. Here we have a good example of Schumann's use of the chord of the diminished seventh on 'Enden' to express a question or doubt. We next have a setting of a poem by Byron in a German version by Julius Körner, 'Aus den hebräischen Gesängen', no. 15. Byron's original 'My soul is dark' speaks of his harp, but the translator has substituted 'Laute'. A gloomy descending passage of chromatic quavers runs through most of the song as the poet bids the minstrel tune his lute to charm away his tears and revive his hopes. The voice ranges over a wide span as he calls for a wilder strain that his heart may either break or be healed. There is here a rare use, at this period, of a diminished third at 'da brech' es' with poignant effect. The postlude dies away to end on a major chord of hope. A second song, 'Rätsel', though ascribed to Byron, is more probably by Catherine Fanshawe, here translated by Karl Kannegiesser. It is an amusing riddle to which the answer is H – or, in German, B natural. The composer gives away the answer in an introductory double octave on B. The song is really only suitable for a German audience.

We now travel to Ireland – or, rather, Italy – for two songs by Thomas Moore in a version by Ferdinand Freiligrath: 'Zwei venetianische Lieder'. The first, 'Row gently here, my gondolier', has a rhythmic figure on the piano suggestive of the rowing of the boatman. The repetition 'Leis, leis, leis' on a diminuendo has a charming effect at the end of the verse. In verse two the lover climbs the beloved's balcony with a rueful remark that if only we took as much trouble over Heaven as we do over women, what angels we should be! The second song, 'When through the Piazzetta', is strophically set, with a gay prelude, followed by a thrumming guitar accompaniment as the poet tells Ninetta that he will come to her at evening. The delicious piano parts are the chief charm of both songs and they are delightful to sing. Two songs by Heine are nos. 21 and 24. No. 21, 'Was will die einsame Träne', is a good example of Schumann's fondness for supertonic harmony, especially, as here, a B minor chord in the key of A major. 'A tear from the past still troubles me, its sisters have all vanished in Night and Wind, like my love.' There is a brief break after 'Nacht' suggesting the vanished sorrows. The song is in ABBA form, an unusual one for Schumann. The other song is one of Schumann's loveliest: 'Du bist wie eine Blume', just a single page but packed with beauty. As in 'Die Lotosblume' the accompaniment has pulsing chords over a steady bass to which the voice enters quietly. The diffidence of the lover is expressed in the long notes on 'Wehmut' and 'mir ist' which hold up the melody. There is an expressive drop of a seventh as the man thinks of laying his hand on the young girl's head while he fervently prays

God to keep her ever sweet and pure. Here the right hand on the piano joins in with its own lovely melody and carries on to the end of the postlude. No. 25, 'Aus den östlichen Rosen', by Rückert, is a charming love-song, light and wistful, full of delightful harmonic touches and an eager melody that is very captivating. In the margin of the manuscript is written 'In Erwartung Claras', 'while expecting Clara'.

There are twenty-six songs in all, and it will be remembered that in the last song of Op. 24 the poet said: 'the pale letters will glow'. So what more suitable song could there be to end the cycle with than 'Zum Schluss'? This is another Rückert lyric. Very solemnly the poem says: 'Here I have woven this imperfect wreath for you, Sister Bride. When God's sunlight shall shine on us, then will the wreath be perfected'. The chords with which the song opens are those of the first arpeggio of 'Widmung' and so the cycle has come full circle with great earnestness. Such was the gift Schumann prepared with so much love and devotion for his bride.

The *Eichendorff* Liederkreis *and* Dichterliebe

In May, after a short visit to Clara in Berlin, Schumann was back in Leipzig where spring was in full bloom and he was full of enthusiasm. The result was the composition, within the space of a single month, of his two greatest masterpieces, the cycles Op. 39 and Op. 48.

The Eichendorff *Liederkreis*, Op. 39, though not strictly a cycle, has a unity of theme; the songs are all romantic in the sense of being in close touch with nature. Birds, flowers, the moon are all symbols of the love theme, all twelve deal with some aspects of romance and its connection with human experience. Keys are linked through a series of changes from F sharp minor to the final F sharp major of the last song.

The first song is 'In der Fremde'. In the story from which the poem was taken, the singer was playing a guitar; this the arpeggiando piano part suggests. In the first few bars the syncopated chords which follow the voice are strongly accented, suggesting the lightning flashes of the storm the exile thinks of as coming from his homeland where his parents have long since died. A melody in the right hand adds sadness to his thoughts of the time when he too will be dead. This is a very moving song with a haunting tune. No. 2, 'Intermezzo', is a typical example of Schumann's predilection for syncopation. Four chords begin the song, but not till the voice comes in is there a single note on the beat. It is a happy love-song. The syncopated left hand is later joined by an independent melody in the right which echoes the one in 'Du bist wie eine Blume':

Ex. 4
(i)

fröh – lich

(ii)

In 'Waldesgespräch', no. 3, we are in a world of fantasy where Schumann can indulge in some pictorial writing. The poem tells of the encounter of a hunter with an enchantress, a woodland witch; we hear the hunting-horn as the rider meets the pale stranger. With no foreboding, he accosts her. A catch in the voice between 'führ' and 'dich heim' is the only indication that something is not quite right. The key abruptly changes, the E on which 'heim' alights being transformed from being the tonic to be the mediant of C major, giving an eerie effect. In plaintive tones the stranger tells of her broken heart and bids the hunter flee from her. But recovering his poise, he admires her beauty, till suddenly realisation dawns upon him and he exclaims 'you are the Lorelei'. Mockingly she repeats his first words, 'It is late, it is cold', then harshly tells him he will never escape from the forest. The postlude goes quietly on its way, reverting to the opening theme. Having swallowed its victim, the forest is unconcerned. After this splendidly dramatic song we have a complete contrast in 'Die Stille', no. 4. It begins without any prelude, a delicate reverie in which the girl tells of her happiness, which nobody save One must know. It has a lovely atmosphere of intimacy and stillness. The next song, 'Mondnacht', is one of Schumann's greatest. Night is portrayed here in its mysterious and magical aspect. A descending phrase in the right hand, repeated in the interludes, leads into shimmering repeated semiquavers; the voice enters in hushed tones on a rising phrase up to the word 'Himmel', then with the descending bass comes down again at the idea of heaven coming down to kiss the earth. A very Schumannesque touch is the clash of E♯ on the word 'hätt' against E natural in the descending bass. The effect of the song is magical if sung with no nuance until the very end where the imagery gives place to the human element. There are differences of opinion as to the execution of the mordents. They appeared in a copy of Schumann's periodical, the *Neue Zeitschrift*, thus:

Ex. 5

However they are performed, they must be absolutely smooth so as not to disturb the stillness.

After these quiet songs comes 'Schöne Fremde', no. 6, another night song, but instead of the holy hush of 'Mondnacht' there is a breeze blowing through the trees. It is the mystery and magic of night under the moon that is the underlying feeling. The poet cries: 'What have you done to me, fantastic night?' He feels as if the gods had returned to the ancient walls, the stars look down and everything speaks to him of great joy to come. The quavers that shimmered in 'Mondnacht' are here broken up and there is movement in the bass. The vocal melody ranges more freely and builds up to a fine climax. The postlude carries on with its own melody in a way that may have been in Brahms's mind when he wrote 'Meine Liebe ist grün'.

'Auf einer Burg', no. 7, begins without prelude in a melody consisting largely of falling fifths and rising sixths. It is devoid of human emotion as it tells of the castle where the old knight has sat for many hundred years and turned at last to stone. A wedding party is in progress, in the valley all are happy, and the pretty bride is weeping – a ritenuto and an end on the dominant, into E major, are the only comment on 'Braut, die weinet' and one is left with the feeling that no one any longer cares. No. 8 is another song of exile, 'In der Fremde'. A little figure opens the song and reappears during it to represent the streamlet or the rustling of trees or the song of the nightingale. The vocal line makes much use of the falling fifths characteristic of the previous song. Nostalgic reminiscence mingles with the present as, half dreaming, the poet sees his beloved waiting for him, and then remembers that she has long been dead. The short phrases induce a dreamlike atmosphere as the poet's thought wavers between past and present, and there is no great expression even at the words 'she is long since dead'. His resignation is nearly complete. In 'Wehmut', no. 9, this resignation is only superficial; when he gladdens his hearers with his happy song, in his heart the tears are flowing. The melody is beautiful and very vocal.

In the next song, 'Zwielicht', no. 10, Schumann has created something quite new in song, an aspect of night as something sinister. The opening bars set the mood:

Ex. 6

Twilight falls and with the coming of darkness treachery is in the air. 'Trust no one, not even your best friend; be on your guard and alert.' This powerful song makes much use of chromaticism, and its whispered ending on low A sharp is very dramatic. One wonders whether Schumann was remembering the dreadful time when Clara, torn between loyalty to her father and to Schumann, suggested postponing any ideas of marriage.

'Im Walde', no. 11, begins with memories of a wedding party, the sound of birds and the horns of hunters, to a lively rhythmic accompaniment. Then suddenly all is silent, night falls and the poet shudders to the depths of his soul. An impressive drop of an octave is an optional and very effective end. After this rather eerie song the cycle comes to an ecstatic end in 'Frühlingsnacht', no. 12. To a cascade of semiquaver triplets the poet welcomes spring; the moon is shining and he does not know whether to laugh or cry. It is unbelievable, but the stars, moon and all nature are shouting: 'She is yours, she is yours.' And so through all the moods of joy and gloom this great work comes to a triumphant end.

Mention must here be made of 'Der frohe Wandersmann', which was intended to be the first song of the *Liederkreis*, but was replaced by the first 'In der Fremde'. It is a song of the road, with a good marching rhythm, but the vocal line is rather square and lacking in charm. It is certainly not up to the standard of the rest of the cycle. It appeared later in Op. 77.

It is amazing that, after this great work, Schumann should have been able to continue with preparation of another great cycle of sixteen songs. He had already dipped into Heine's *Buch der Lieder* and familiarised himself with his poetic style; his own style and technique he had perfected in the Eichendorff songs, he was now ready for the supreme test of his genius. He had been through a period of great suffering and frustration and he was ripe to find inspiration in these poems, which probed the heart of a lover's experience. Heine's intensity and economy were well matched in the music, and though some of the bitter irony may have escaped him, the result of this partnership was to be the crown of his achievement.

Dichterliebe, Op. 48, is dedicated to Wilhelmine Schröder-Devrient, who became famous when, not quite eighteen, she sang Leonora in the revival of Beethoven's *Fidelio*. The cycle begins 'Im wunderschönen Monat Mai', 'In lovely May I fell in love, in lovely May I told my love and longing'. From the outset, even in this apparently happy poem, the doubts and uncertainties of love are foreshadowed by questioning arpeggios of the introduction in F♯ minor leading to the happy A major of the vocal entry, only to be contradicted at the return to the minor in interlude and postlude with the questioning dominant seventh on which it ends. If tears were not far away at the close, they now actually fall in 'Aus meinen Tränen spriessen', but from them will spring flowers, and from his sighs a chorus of nightingales. All these he will send to her if she will only love him. Here is Heine's use of nature as symbolic of love, which aroused so ready a response in Schumann. Now all doubts are laid aside as in 'Die Rose, die Lilie, die Taube, die Sonne' all that he had loved in nature are now surpassed by the 'One' and only love. To a tripping accompaniment of semiquavers the singer has scarcely time for breath in this exuberantly happy little song. The lovers are together in no. 4, 'Wenn ich in deine Augen seh' '. In quasi-recitative the lover gazes into the beloved's eyes, simple chords echo the voice, then build up to a climax at the kiss which heals all wounds. It is heaven to lie on her breast, but when she says 'I love you' he must weep bitterly. Heine obviously distrusts her sincerity. Did Schumann ignore the imputation? He would be quite capable of weeping either for joy or at his own unworthiness. On the other hand, does that diminished seventh on 'sprichst', taken together with the wavering tonality of the postlude, mean that he understood Heine's meaning? It is for the singer to decide and interpret accordingly.

'Ich will meine Seele tauchen' is an extreme example of Heine's nature symbolism. Through the imagery of the song trembling in the cup of the lily the poet thinks of the kiss that the beloved gave him in a wonderful hour. The piano has a demisemiquaver figure under a right-hand tune in falling thirds, all giving a suggestion of the trembling kiss and only the little acciaccaturas in the postlude suggest that all is not well.

Without prelude the voice enters in 'Im Rhein, im heiligen Strome', in a wonderful sound-picture of the river in which is mirrored the great cathedral of Cologne. Deep octaves suggest the cathedral, while over them flows the river in long continuous descending waves. For a moment the figures are reversed as in thought we enter the cathedral to see the old picture which, in time of trouble, had been so comforting. Outside again the mirror image returns as the lover reflects on the likeness of the picture to his beloved. A long postlude carries the river out of our sight.

By now the break between the lovers is final, in 'Ich grolle nicht' the poet emphatically, too emphatically, protests that he bears no grudge. His resignation is belied by the repeated quaver chords (so often associated with heart-beats). He knows that the beloved is as unhappy as he is for all her diamonds. In dreams he sees 'the snake feed upon her breast'. The high alternative notes do not appear in the original manuscript but were added to the proof. They certainly seem a logical climax to the progression and appear in the piano part. 'Und wüssten's die Blumen, die kleinen' has a tremolando accompaniment that for the most part follows the voice melody. The lover appeals to the flowers and nightingales: if only they knew how deeply he is wounded, they would try to console him. Only 'One' knows it, and she it is who has broken his heart. On the powerful word 'zerrissen' the tremolando stops and is replaced by two stabbing chords, followed by a wildly passionate postlude. In 'Das ist ein Flöten und Geigen' the jealous lover is looking in at a wedding-feast and sees the beloved happily dancing and fancies he can hear the angels weep. A continuous melody in the right hand is accompanied by a rhythmic stamping in the bass, as the noisy dance continues right to the end of the song with a long postlude. It will be interesting to compare this song with 'Der Spielmann', Op. 40, no. 4. In no. 10, 'Hör' ich das Liedchen klingen', the poor man is tormented by a tune the beloved used to sing; we first hear it on the piano in syncopation, then the voice has it. It will not go, though it makes him wild with distress. He goes to the wooded hills to escape and there relieve his heart with tears, but even there it follows him. The postlude carries on with it and gradually it passes out of our hearing.

In bitter mood he reflects on the topsy-turviness of life in 'Ein Jüngling liebt ein Mädchen', no. 11. A young man loves a girl who has chosen another, who loves yet another and has married her. In pique the girl takes the first man to come along. This is sad for the young man. It is an old story but ever new and it breaks the heart of the man to whom it happens. To a jaunty, almost brutal, accompaniment the singer tells the story quite dispassionately, with only a slight softening at 'der Jüngling ist übel d'ran', and a bitter ritardando at the last 'dem bricht das Herz entzwei'.

'Am leuchtenden Sommermorgen', 'One lovely summer morning', he walks in the garden. A prelude of descending arpeggios moves from an augmented sixth to the key of B flat major. The flowers whisper together, but he cannot hear them. They look at him with pity. Then there is a magical change to G major as they whisper to him, 'Do not be hard on our sister, you pale man', with a very moving touch as the piano has the arpeggio of the opening bar of the song on 'blasser'. A long and lovely postlude follows.

All his early life Heine had been subject to dreams, and now follow two contrasted ones. The first, 'Ich hab' im Traum geweinet', is all in recitative, interrupted by a grim drum-beat. It is in E flat minor, a key often associated with death in Schumann's songs. He dreams his love is in her grave, he wakes and weeps; then that she has left him. Still faster flow his tears. Finally, and here the piano joins the voice, he dreams she still loves him. He wakes and his tears fall in a flood. Here the voice rises to the highest pitch accompanied by chromatic chords. Then silence and another drum figure and two short final chords. The nightmare effect shows Schumann's insight into the neurotic mind of the poet. The other dream-song is 'Allnächtlich im Traume'. Where the impression of the previous dream was clear-cut and definite, in this one it is confused. It is all in short phrases and has no prelude. Now his tears are only in the dream. He dreams that she receives him kindly and he sinks sobbing at her feet. For one bar the 2/4 time changes to 3/4 as he flings himself towards her and a descending passage brings him to his knees. The beloved also weeps and hands him a wreath of cypress, and a gentle word. Abruptly he wakes, there is no wreath and he has forgotten what she said. The short phrases and sudden changes of rhythm all add to the blurred effect of the dream. Can one think that he is beginning to recover? Some singers make much of the 'hab' ich vergessen', but there is no expression mark beyond a crescendo up to the word 'Wort' and the end is very abrupt indeed. The suggestion that recovery is beginning is strengthened by the next song, no. 15, 'Aus alten Märchen'. The poet thinks of a fairy-tale land where wonders never cease and all is blissful. A lively march rhythm continues throughout in a cheerful manner, lightened a little for the coloured flowers and blue lights flashing from leaf and flower. The music builds up to a climax in a string of dominant sevenths as his imagination runs riot, then suddenly with 'Ach, ach!' he realises how unattainable such bliss is. The tempo slows as sadly he reflects and the vision dissolves like bubbles. Very softly the postlude has the original theme but this time in staccato chords; then a few sustained chords end the song. Now the poet is determined to free himself from his obsession and he sets about it with grim humour in 'Die alten bösen Lieder'. A bold C sharp minor chord followed by declamatory octaves indicates that his mind is made up. 'An end to all this' he seems to say. Let us bury these bad old songs in a coffin larger than the cask at Heidelberg, on a bier longer than the bridge at Mainz, and with twelve giants stronger than St Christopher in Cologne Cathedral to carry it.

The theme:

Ex. 7

Fairly slow

Die al - ten, bö - sen Lie - der, die Träu - me bös' und arg,

persists throughout in various keys until the giants take up the coffin, when it changes to single crotchet chords in a slow, heavy funeral march. At a sforzando chord of a diminished seventh the coffin crashes into the sea. Very quietly he asks: 'Do you know why the coffin must be so large and heavy?' A portamento carries the voice up an octave to C sharp, which then, by one of Schumann's beautiful key-changes, becomes the leading-note of D major. 'Because,' the poet answers, 'in it are buried all my love and sorrow.' In this one line is crystallised all the anguish that has been endured throughout the sixteen songs. The piano now glides into the melody of 'Am leuchtenden Sommermorgen', then winds its way through nearly a page of arabesques. It is hard not to imagine Schumann at the piano, loath to let the great work leave his hands. Finally the work comes to its end in blessed peace.

Lovely songs were still to come from his pen, but never again that complete fusion of poetry and music in such a sustained form and with such psychological insight into a poet's mind. Had he never written another note he would still have gone down to posterity as one of the greatest song-writers.

Four songs written at this period were intended for the cycle but later rejected. 'Dein Angesicht', Op. 127, no. 2, is a dream-song. The lover sees his beloved's face, sweet but pale. Only her lips are red – here a modulation from E flat major to G major is followed by an ominous flattening of the leading-note at 'Death will kiss them white'. The song is beautiful, only slightly marred by the repetition of the opening lines at the end of the poem. No. 3,

'Es leuchtet meine Liebe', tells a curious tale of a knight and his lady overtaken by the giant of the wilderness. The maiden flees, the knight is killed and the giant stumps off home. A little figure

♩ ♫ ♩ for the killing of the knight reminds us a little of

another giant, Fafner, killing his brother in *Das Rheingold*. A small point worth noting is the use of 'Ritter' instead of 'Riese' at the giant's first appearance.

Two songs later to appear as Op. 142, nos. 2 and 4, are 'Lehn' deine Wang'', which is not very interesting, and 'Mein Wagen rollet langsam', which is. This was at one time thought to be Schumann's last song. It was in fact written in May 1840. It is another of Heine's dream phantasies and has a descriptive setting. We hear the jolting carriage in a figure on the piano:

Ex. 8

Nach dem Sinn des Gedichts (*Following the sense of the poem*)

on its way through wooded country. Ex. 8 changes as the poet sits and dreams of his beloved. The carriage jogs on, then suddenly three shadowy figures steal in. The vocal line is broken up as the figures try to attract his attention, grimacing, tittering and swirling like mists; and then to a cascade of sixths they titter and fade away. The long postlude describes the poet's thoughts as the carriage jolts away out of sight. This song might well have done for *Dichterliebe* but perhaps it was felt to be too long.

Songs by Various Poets

There are a number of songs for which there are no precise dates, or which definitely belong to the early months of the year 1840. A setting of Robert Burns's 'A red, red rose' or 'Dem roten Röslein gleicht mein Lieb' was probably written at the same time as the eight Burns lyrics in the Eichendorff *Liederkreis*. If one were not so wedded to the traditional setting we could find this one quite attractive with its falling fifths in the voice, and right hand on the piano in contrary motion with the left. It is no. 2 of Op. 27. No. 1 is 'Sag an, o lieber Vogel mein' to words by Christian Hebbel. This may belong to an even earlier date as it shows little sign of the mastery by now acquired by the composer. No. 3 is by Chamisso, 'Was soll ich sagen'; it conveys the misgivings of an older man at accepting the love of a young girl. Chamisso was thirty-eight when he married a girl of eighteen. Was Schumann perhaps remembering the evening when he first kissed the sixteen-year-old Clara whom he had hitherto regarded just as a dear child? It is written in very short phrases which suggest the man's diffidence. No. 4, 'Jasminenstrauch' by Rückert, is a lovely little song. In a marginal note the composer says that this is an attempt to find music for the stirrings of nature and the symbolism of human love. The jasmine was green when it went to sleep – gentle waving of leaves is suggested by semiquaver groups on the piano – at the first breath of morning it was snow-white. 'What has happened?' the bush asks on an arpeggio of the diminished seventh. 'That is what happens to trees when they dream in spring.' This delightful miniature should be heard more often. The fifth and last song of Op. 27 was written much later but it is convenient to consider it here. 'Nur ein lächelnder Blick' by Georg Zimmermann is very sentimental and proved rather a pitfall for Schumann. It has a delightful melody repeated to such excess that it gets wearisome before the end.

The songs of Op. 51 include Rückert's delightful 'Volksliedchen'. The composer thought highly of it and it was twice published singly before being added to Op. 51. To a tripping accompaniment the girl comes out into the garden in her green hat. Her first thought is of her lover. The simple poem has an equally simple setting, but with delightful touches such as the staccato accompaniment as she walks, which becomes legato when she thinks of her lover, and the warmth of her 'mein erster Gedanke' and the catch in her breath at the last 'was nun mein Liebster tut', between 'mein' and 'Liebster'. A delicious postlude takes her tripping on her way. No. 3, 'Ich wand're nicht' by Carl Christern, was written at a time when Robert and Clara had thought of eloping in order to escape her father's ban on their marriage. 'Why should I travel to foreign lands when my home-land is so fair? The skies may be bright, but my love's smile is brighter.' In a letter Schumann told Clara that the music is 'the Scherzino in another form'. The two opening bars transform bars 11–13 of the Scherzo of the *Klavierstücke*, Op. 32, no. 1, written in 1839. The song is delightfully fresh and straightforward with the piano answering the singer's phrases. It is strophic, and grateful to sing because of its warmth and good range.

By the end of March Schumann had composed some forty songs and a rest was imperative. However, by April he was back at work on songs for Op. 53. No. 1 is 'Blondels Lied' by Johann Seidl, the poet of Schubert's last song 'Die Taubenpost'. It is in ballad style and tells the story of Richard I and his faithful minstrel who sought and found him when he had been held to ransom by Leopold of Austria. It is really too long for public performance. No. 2 is a setting of a poor poem by Wilhelmine Lorenz called 'Lorelei'. More interesting is a little drama by Heine called 'Der arme Peter' I, II and III. Two jangling chords set the scene with their suggestion of a hurdy-gurdy. A village dance is in progress. Poor Peter stands alone, watching his beloved dancing with his rival Hans, her bridegroom. He muses: 'Were I not a reasonable chap I would do myself an injury.' No. II opens with a pathetic E minor triad. At once we know that his reasonableness is not very strong. He cannot face Grete, he is too shy. So he goes off to the mountains to weep. Still the dance tune runs in his head, or rather on the piano in the postlude. In III he has become so pale that the girls all ask 'Has he come from the grave?' 'No,' the neighbours answer, 'he is on the way to it.' The last few bars with their suggestion of a funeral march can be taken literally or ironically. After all, Heine himself did not die of love, he buried it as we know from *Dichterliebe*. Another poem by him is in an unusual vein. We know that he fought against his impulse to write of flowers and dreams of love and so would set himself to write of other things as an exercise. 'Abends am Strand', Op. 45, no. 3, is one. A party of friends are watching, from the shore, a ship on the sea. A flowing figure suggests the lapping of the waves. They see the lights come on in the lighthouse and they talk of distant lands. The piano describes the different lands with varying touches. Heine's comic account of the 'dirty Laplanders' with their high-pitched cries is taken up by Schumann with a prolonged 'schrei'n' high in the voice. After a return to the first theme the watchers fall silent, the ship is now out of sight. This is a song well worth singing.

Two more Heine songs in ballad form belong to this period. The well-known 'Die beiden Grenadiere', Op. 49, no. 1, is the more successful. Heine had a great admiration for Napoleon, as had Schumann. This is the story of two grenadiers making their way home, prisoners of war released from Russia. A bugle call and drum roll introduce them; a descending octave passage in the bass expresses their weariness, though a drum roll reveals that their spirit is not quite broken. When they learn that the war has been lost and Napoleon captured, they weep. The two men are well contrasted, the practical one, determined to get home, and the idealistic hero-worshipper with no more will to struggle now his hero has been taken. But when he dies, he begs his comrade to let him be buried in French soil with his musket at his side, till the cannon's roar shall awaken the dead and – to the sound of the 'Marseillaise' – he will rise from the grave to guard the Emperor. Finally there is a slow progression of chords as death overtakes him. The ballad form is not one in which Schumann is generally successful but this story has caught his imagination and produced a great song. The other ballad, 'Die feindlichen Brüder', is not comparable. It tells of two brothers who fought for the hand of the Countess Laura. The treatment is in straightforward ballad style, softening to a more lyrical style for the Countess, who cannot decide between them. The brothers fight to the death. Many centuries later the castle has gone, but at midnight the sound of clashing swords is heard in the valley. There is not much variety or drama in the music and it would need a very skilful and dramatic singer to make it effective.

Chamisso and Frauenliebe und -leben

After this great spate of composition it is not surprising that
Schumann had to rest for a time. Clara had returned to Leipzig
and the law case for permission to marry was before the courts.
It was not till July that Schumann resumed song-writing. What
was more natural than that he should feel drawn to poems about
the life and love of a young woman, when to him 'woman' meant
Clara? So his next work was *Frauenliebe und -leben* to poems by
Chamisso, Op. 42. This is an intimate account of a woman's life.
Here were no problems of irony or neurosis as in Heine, but
straightforward poetry of a kind to give the composer scope for
sentiment. To modern taste, the woman in these poems is really
too much of a doormat, but we have to put ourselves back into
the period in which they were written if we are not to miss some
music of great beauty. Clara was some nine years younger than
Schumann and she had looked up to him from the time she was
a little girl, so there was nothing unnatural to either of them in
the very humble attitude of the woman of the poems. We must
also bear in mind the position of women at that time, especially in
Germany, so different from what it is now. The singer today must
put aside her modern ideas and try to imagine herself a woman of
the early nineteenth century if she is to sing these songs con-
vincingly. Chamisso's poetry may not be of the finest quality but
it is expressive and perfectly attuned to Schumann's music.

No. 1, 'Seit ich ihn gesehen': the heroine has just seen the hero.
She is dazzled by his appearance and blind to everything and
everyone else. There is a lovely phrase for 'wie in wachen Traume'
which is spoiled if a crescendo to the top note on 'wachen' is
indulged in. The idea of the man's image diving into her darkness
is suggested by the drop of a seventh on 'tiefstem'. The last three
bars of the verse are quoted in the slow movement of the B flat
symphony of 1841. The song is in strophic form and in the second
verse the girl's one desire is to creep away to her own room and
weep. No. 2, 'Er, der Herrlichste von Allen', tells us why she must
weep. He is the most wonderful man and quite unattainable. The
reiterated chords express her beating heart, and in the interludes
the piano takes up her opening phrase. She compares him to an
unattainable star in the sky and she turns the knife in her wound

by promising to bless the woman he will find worthy of his love, even if it breaks her heart. A plaintive little figure of a minim descending to a crotchet on the piano suggests the pain her unselfishness causes her. The song ends with a reprise of the first verse, ending with 'he is so gentle and so good'. The next song begins without any prelude, 'Ich kann's nicht fassen, nicht glauben': the impossible has happened. The voice breaks out in blank astonishment. She cannot believe it, she must be dreaming. Short stabbing chords emphasise her bewilderment. But she reassures herself with the memory of his words: 'ich bin auf ewig dein'. So, if it is only a dream, 'let me die, dreaming, in his arms, in endless bliss'. Again she repeats her amazement that from all others he should have chosen her. Now she is officially betrothed and in no. 4, 'Du Ring an meinem Finger', she contemplates her ring in quiet rapture. Here the direction *Innig* is very appropriate. She is talking to herself and thinking how her betrothal has opened her eyes to a new world of endless worth. She dedicates herself to the service of her husband in whose light alone she can shine. At the suggestion of submission and service the music has a falling interval, here on 'ihm leben'. It occurred in no. 2 where she promised to bless her rival, and we shall meet it again in the next song. The accompaniment is gently flowing except when the thought of dedication warms it up into repeated quaver chords. No. 5, 'Helft mir, ihr Schwestern', is all bustle and commotion. It is her wedding day and she is being dressed for the ceremony. She does not know whether to laugh or to cry. The arpeggios on the piano remind us of the opening bars of 'Widmung' in Op. 39. As the sisters wind her myrtle wreath she has a moment of stupid fear: her lover was so impatient for this day! But she wants to be clear-eyed to meet him, so she must not weep. Again she dedicates herself to him, then tearfully bids her sisters 'Goodbye'. Her last words are very cleverly put low down in the voice, giving the suggestion of unshed tears. The postlude delightfully suggests a wedding march as she goes off. She is now married. No. 6, 'Süsser Freund', is the most difficult for a modern woman to accept. It takes our heroine twenty-three bars of slow tempo to tell her husband that she is going to have a baby and even then it is the piano that has to tell him. Over a very slight chordal accompaniment in quasi-recitative she asks her husband why he cannot understand her fits of crying. She is so frightened and yet so happy if only she could find words to tell him. Let him come and hold her tight in his arms and she will whisper in his ear. This the piano does for her in the chords of the first bars of the song. Very excitedly, over repeated chords in the piano, she hugs her husband and says 'now you can understand my tears'. In music of the opening page she now talks freely of the baby to come and plans where the cradle shall stand when her happy dream is fulfilled and her husband's little replica shall smile back at her. After a short interlude the song ends with her soft sigh 'dein Bildnis'. Two chords introduce no. 7, 'An meinem Herzen, an meiner Brust'. She is all mother as she talks to her baby, over a rocking figure on the piano. She sings of her happiness, a happiness that only a mother can know. She pities poor men who can never enjoy such bliss. On the last page the arpeggios change to short chords as she catches up the child and hugs it. The postlude has a lovely curving melody which suggests the mother lifting the baby up and down. If some of the poems have seemed sentimental, and tolerable only for the lovely music that clothes them, the last one is as stark and true to life as possible, and Schumann's setting is a masterpiece of economy: 'Nun hast du mir den ersten Schmerz getan'. The triad of D minor which begins the song is surely one of the most poignant chords in music. We have a vivid picture of a stricken woman, dry-eyed, gazing at her husband's dead body. In recitative low in the voice she accuses him of hurting her for the first time and mortally. Now the world is empty. The pitch rises to the word 'leer' (empty) and descends again to the end of the song. The sforzando chord on 'leer' makes it sound chill and empty and the tragic chromaticism makes it infinitely moving. The curtain falls; there lies her happiness, 'du, meine Welt'. There is a long pause, then the piano postlude takes her back to the first time she saw the man who was to be her all, with a repetition of the music of the first song of the cycle. Whatever one may feel about the poet's contribution, no one can doubt the complete sincerity of the composer. As in *Dichterliebe* he had had the insight to enter into the complexities of Heine's verse, so here his warm sympathy has enabled him to enter with understanding the mind and heart of a young girl and her development through marriage, motherhood, maturity and widowhood, and clothe it with unforgettable music.

Chamisso also provides the texts of three ballads about women, Op. 31. The first is 'Die Löwenbraut'. This grisly story about a girl and her favourite lion has some picturesque touches but is too long to sustain our interest. Schumann's dramatic gifts are not enough to keep a long story vivid. He has some pictorial touches for the lion's dignified gait and savage growls when the bridegroom comes to fetch his bride from the cage, where she is bidding the lion goodbye, but her long narrative to snatches of 'Widmung' hold up the action too long for even the chromatic chords at the climax to compensate. 'Die Kartenlegerin' is much more successful. The theme is light and varied and Schumann responds with many picturesque touches. The text is a translation from the French of Béranger. While her mother sleeps, a girl puts down her knitting and takes up a pack of cards. A light motif, which anticipates the dealing of cards in Bizet's *Carmen*, opens the song. We are taken through various readings, each with appropriate music; every time the girl thinks something good turns up another card dashes her hopes. Finally, a horrible woman appears to ruin her happiness – at which moment her mother wakes up and scolds her. Ruefully the girl exclaims, 'The cards certainly do not lie!' This is a delightful song and we get a charming picture of the silly girl and her fortune-telling. The third song, 'Die rote Hanna', also translated from Béranger, is rather long with an optional chorus and to the present writer not very interesting.

Besides translating from French the gifted and much-travelled Chamisso had also made some versions of lyrics by the Danish poet Hans Andersen. Four of these were set by Schumann, with one from modern Greek, and form Op. 40. No. 1, 'Märzveilchen', is a charming tale of a young man, on a frosty morning, looking at the flower pattern made on a window-pane. Behind the window are two laughing violet eyes. Warm breath will melt the frost and then 'Heaven help the young man'. A dainty staccato tune in syncopation is taken up by the voice on the beat in a melody which lingers on the word 'Augenpaar'. The little joke is repeated and a gay postlude ends the song. It is a really delightful miniature. No. 2 has a very Scandinavian theme. Entitled 'Muttertraum', it tells of the mother brooding happily over her baby son's cradle. But the introduction should have warned us that all is not well. It is the theme we have met in 'Zwielicht' (Ex. 6) for in verse two

the ravens are croaking outside her window saying, 'Your ange
will grow up to be a thief and the robber will serve us for meat.
The accompaniment continues the sinister theme to the end of th
postlude. The third song is a pathetic tale of a young soldier
'Der Soldat'. He is marching wearily to the sound of muffle
drums, to the place where he and eight others in a firing squa
are appointed to shoot his best friend. The men prepare to fire
but of the nine, eight bullets missed because the men wer
trembling so much, only 'I, I shot him through the heart'. Thi
last is whispered over a tremolando on the piano. The postlud
suggests the sagging body of the victim. A tragic and touchin
song, short enough not to strain Schumann's dramatic powers

No. 4 is 'Der Spielmann'. It is interesting to compare this wit
two other wedding songs. The vocal melody recalls 'Im Walde
Op. 39, no. 11, and the fiddle-playing and dance themes 'Das is
ein Flöten und Geigen' in *Dichterliebe*. In this song the fiddle is no
continuous but echoes the voice, to a continuous dance rhythr
in the bass. The noisy playing quietens as the narrator describe
the deathlike pallor of the bride, 'dead for him she does not forget
who at the party is not the bridegroom. He stands in their mids
and plays his fiddle gaily enough.' Then after a crashing chord th
fiddler clutches his fiddle and plays more wildly. His hair turn
grey and he wildly tears at the strings. Suddenly the tune stops
only the stamping bass continues. 'I will not watch, it will driv
me mad!' He exclaims, 'But why do you point at me?' The ke
changes and in slow tempo he prays, 'O God, don't let anyone g
mad. I too am a poor musician.' The music dies away in a lon
postlude. This is a truly remarkable song and worthy of being sun
more often. The last song of the set is a complete contrast; it is th
one translated from Greek, 'Verratene Liebe', an enchanting littl
song. Two lovers kissed when no one was there to see, but a sta
dropped from the sky and told the sea, who told the rudder, whic
told the helmsman, who told his sweetheart. Now every boy an
girl in the street is singing about it. The accompaniment is ver
light, at first leaving the voice unsupported, then it graduall
builds up until it is quite full and rich when the news reaches th
boys and girls. The charming postlude ends with a delightful littl
scale passage – or, rather, chromatically decorated arpeggio.

End of the Wonderful Year

he last songs of the year begin with *Six Poems from a Painter's ng-book* by Robert Reinick, Op. 36. 'Sonntags am Rhein' scribes a Sunday-morning walk beside the Rhine, with church lls ringing and a ship on the water; all is happiness and piety. he vocal line is charming and wide-ranging and at one point the ss has a melody in canon. The reiterated chordal accompaniment oves into the treble clef giving an organ effect as the people me out of church. No. 2, 'Ständchen', is a more or less con-ntional serenade poem but set to enchanting music in strophic rm, with a guitar-like accompaniment; a song well worth the nger's notice. No. 3 is 'Nichts schöneres', 'When first they met thought he had never known anything more beautiful than to ze into her eyes, to kiss and eventually to make her his wife.' ow could such words fail to inspire the composer to a very tractive setting? The opening bar makes one wonder whether ugo Wolf remembered it when he wrote 'Erste Begegnung'. he fourth song, 'An den Sonnenschein', is the 'O sunny beam' hich we all sang in our childhood. It is in folk-song style and as a great favourite with the Swedish singer Jenny Lind. No. 5 a strange song, 'Dichters Genesung'. The queen of the elves mes to the poet on a moonlight night to tempt him away from s earthly body to come and live with her in the land of dreams. am she,' she sings, 'of whom you have often dreamed and sung.' remolando chords describe the dance of the elves and the queen's pearance. However, when morning comes the poet decides he ill find another love, pure and guileless. The song ends with the entical chords that end 'Waldesgespräch', Op. 39, no. 3, which lls of a much more powerful temptress. One wonders if this ng is meant as a bridegroom's farewell to thoughts unbecoming a married man? The last song is 'Liebesbotschaft', on the anuscript of which appear the words, 'the day of the second ading of the banns of marriage'. On 12 August the young uple were given the final judgement of the court and were now ee to go ahead with their plans for the wedding. On the 24th humann wrote to Clara saying that she was to expect a love-tter, probably in music. If this is the one it is certainly ideal for s purpose. It is virtually a piano piece with words, so she could play or sing it as she pleased. The melody is very singable and the words are what one would expect.

After these love-songs come three songs about men in rather lighter vein by Emmanuel Geibel, Op. 30. 'Der Knabe mit der Wunderhorn' is a delightfully gay song with a splendid tune and many of Schumann's favourite horn calls. No. 2, 'Der Page', is very attractive musically with an interesting vocal line, but the page is really too humble. He is prepared to serve his mistress in any and every capacity even to the length of escorting her to her lover and keeping watch outside the door while they kiss. Only a ritenuto at 'du Andre küssest' indicates a slight reluctance on his part. The last of the three is 'Der Hidalgo', which has the rather odd direction 'Etwas kokett', which presumably means that the nobleman's boasting is not to be taken too seriously. He goes out on his horse at night with his sword and his mandoline ready for danger or pleasure, to fight or to serenade the ladies. The accompaniment is in bolero rhythm with a thrumming for the mandoline, and it has a delightful tune which Mahler may have had in mind in the tenor's third song of *Das Lied von der Erde*:

Ex. 9

Es ist so süss zu sche – rzen

The key changes with a graceful easing of the thrumming for the ladies of Seville and there is a falling phrase for the dropping of rose petals on the hero from some lady's balcony. At the thought of danger the key reverts to D major and the song ends gaily with the boast that he will come home with either flowers or wounds.

This is a delightful song and full of high spirits, splendid for a tenor or high baritone. One more Geibel setting belongs to this exciting month of August. 'Sehnsucht', Op. 51, no. 1, begins with a torrent of demisemiquavers in alternating octaves. The voice enters after a brief pause, to an accompaniment of quaver chords in triplets. It has a fine driving melody as the poet bewails the narrow life of the North. Here a chilly touch is given by an accented D flat on the piano. He longs to escape to warmer climes and there is a lovely effect as the minor changes to major on 'wohl leuchtet die Ferne'. There is a quotation from Schubert's 'Der Wanderer' at 'kann nicht hin'. Youth is passing and time is fleeting is the theme of the song. Another torrent of demisemiquavers ends the song as it began. This must have startled the Leipzigers at the time and Schumann admitted that it was unusual.

On 12 September, the eve of Clara's twenty-first birthday, the long waiting was over and the couple were married. It was November before song-writing was renewed with Eichendorff's 'Der Schatzgräber', Op. 45, no. 1. A man is digging furiously for treasure at dead of night when all the world is asleep; an evocative scale passage vividly suggests the motion of digging. The piano part changes to arpeggiando quavers at the words 'God's angels are singing the while, in the calm night'. Suddenly the gleam of red metal catches the man's eyes. Furiously he digs, muttering 'Und wirst du mein, mein'. Deeper and deeper he digs till the rocks come crashing down over the fool. Still he digs; a clatter of mocking laughter echoes in the shaft in a figure of staccato thirds in contrary motion. Sadly the angels' song echoes in the air. Unceasing digging brings the song to a close. This is a remarkable song which deserves to be heard more often. A 'Frühlingsfahrt' of no especial interest follows.

A beautiful setting of 'Die Nonne' by Abraham Fröhlich joins the two ballads in Op. 49 as no. 3. A nun stands in the garden among the roses and watches a bride in the house at her wedding feast. Schumann contrives an organ-like effect for the introduction and the nun. The key changes from D flat major to C sharp minor for a cheerful tune describing the girl in the house. The girl comes to the window to cool her hot cheeks and the nun – now back in D flat major – compares the bride, rosy beneath her white bridal wreath, with herself, pale amid the red roses, pale and joyless.

The word 'Freudenlose' is pathetic over the unresolved dominant seventh with which the song ends. Another sad song is 'Mädchen-Schwermut', published posthumously as Op. 142, no. 3. It is a picture of despair very economically set and quite touching.

In a set of twelve songs, Op. 35, to texts by Justinus Kerner, Schumann returned to a poet five of whose poems he had used in the earliest songs of 1827–8. Their only link is a certain key sequence. No. 1 is 'Lust der Sturmnacht'. Like Lucretius, the poet contrasts the rain and storm outside and congratulates himself on hearing it in the comfortable warmth indoors. Syncopated chords and octave scale passages work up quite good storm effects and the vocal line is very fine. No. 2, 'Stirb, Lieb' und Freud' ', is written for tenor. From a house in Augsburg a girl enters the cathedral. She kneels and prays to the Virgin to be accepted. Unaware of the lily wreath glowing on her head, she approaches the High Altar. All the congregation marvel at the brightness on her hair. 'Take me,' she prays, 'to be a nun, die love and joy.' The man watching her prays, 'God give her peace, she is my beloved, though she does not know it. Die love and light!' This is a striking song of great beauty. The continuous right-hand tune illustrates her unwavering progress up to the final dedication; the heavy octaves in the bass remind us of those in the *Dichterliebe* song, no. 6, here depicting the cathedral bell. Solemn chords change the scene to the man watching from the aisle. As always, young womanhood draws the best from Schumann's tender heart. 'Wanderlied' is a gay and vigorous song in folk-style. 'Erstes Grün' has a delightful melody expressing delight at the coming of spring. Especially attractive is the delicious lilt of the piano part. No. 5, 'Sehnsucht nach der Waldgegend', tells of a man exiled from forest country and forced to live in broad meadowland. He sings nostalgically, to an arpeggiando accompaniment, of the birds and waters of his homeland, but here all is silent and even the birds sing half-heartedly. We are told that Brahms much admired this song. No. 6, 'Auf das Trinkglass eines verstorbenen Freundes', was written in memory of the poet's friend and patron. The death in early life of Schumann's own loved friend Ludwig Schunke a few years earlier must have been in his mind when he set this moving song. In a tune not unlike a chorale the poet addresses the empty glass that once his friend had used. The ritual of white magic is gone through. He fills the glass with German wine and gazes into it. A strange passage in octaves accompanies the voice, 'What I saw in your depths is not to be spoken of to the general'. He drinks; midnight sounds; the glass is empty. Still sounds that note from its crystal depth. Schumann achieves a wonderful atmosphere of magic that is very moving. In 'Wanderung' a horn call is heard and the traveller is on his way. This gay, light-hearted song is a pleasant relief after the charged atmosphere of the previous one. The prelude and postlude of no. 8, 'Stille Liebe', are close quotations from Schubert's 'Dass sie hier gewesen'. The poet bewails his unworthiness to sing his beloved's praises adequately and this is why he sings this little song. It is a subject that could appeal to Schumann, who was so humble where Clara was concerned, and the result is very attractive. No. 9, 'Frage', has no pre- or postlude but serves as a bridge between nos. 8 and 10. 'Without the beauty of flowers and birds and evening light, what could fill a troubled heart with joy?' The piano follows the vocal line closely. The ending, *adagio*, on the dominant of the relative minor seems to throw some doubt on the answer to the question. No. 10, 'Stille Tränen', begins with staccato crotchet chords in 6/4 time over a slow sustained bass and continues throughout almost the entire song. The voice has an opulent melody of great sweep, wonderful to sing for a singer with good breath capacity and control. 'You have awakened from sleep to a heavenly blue sky. While you were happily sleeping the sky was weeping. So many a man weeps at night from grief and in the morning appears to be gay.' This is a very singable song in spite of being rather overloaded with a long interlude and postlude.

The last two songs of Op. 35 have almost identical settings. One wonders why. The music for the first song does not quite so well suit the words of the second one; yet, sung together, the second song seems to gain an added poignancy from the use of the previously heard tune. In 'Wer machte dich so krank?' the sufferer is asked the reason for being so ill. He replies that nothing in nature has harmed him, rather is she the healer. No, it is man who will not let him rest. A lovely effect is the progression at 'keine Sternen Nacht' which suddenly at 'Kein Schatten' turns from E flat major to G flat major – then gradually works back to A flat for the last song, 'Alte Laute'. Here he speaks to his own heart and asks himself why nature cannot wake him from his evil dream. All he hears are the old sounds of a young man's heart, who trusted the world and its pleasure. Those days are past and only an angel can waken him. The music stops here without any postlude and, strangely, is the more moving for lack of it.

Two more Kerner poems were written at this time but not published till later, 'Sängers Trost', Op. 127, no. 1, and 'Trost im Gesang', Op. 142, no. 1.

At various times Robert and Clara had collaborated on some poems from their friend Rückert's *Liebesfrühling*. Some were duets, some were by Clara, some showed signs of collaboration. They were published as Op. 37 as a gift to Clara for her birthday. They were intended to be songs of a light kind and only Robert's own solo songs need be considered here. The first, 'Der Himmel hat eine Träne geweint', is a fanciful song. The sky wept a tear, which, becoming enclosed in a shell, became a pearl. The poet prays that he may enclose his beloved in his arms as a pearl and keep her safe. This sentimental little song is very charming with a haunting tune. No. 3, 'O ihr Herren', is a delightful miniature; a single page, in which a nightingale begs for a place in the gardens of the rich, which she will repay with her singing. It has a very dainty postlude. No. 5, 'Ich hab in mich gesogen', is quite attractive. The lover feels spring in his heart, his loved one is close and between them is a God-given springtime of love. These words would be sure to appeal to the happy young couple, and the piano part rather suggests that Clara had a hand in its composition. No. 6, 'Liebste, was kann denn uns scheiden?', is a strophic song in the form of an optional duet. It is quite attractive, with great play on the rhymes of the poem, but it is too slight for four verses. In no. 8, 'Flügel, Flügel! um zu fliegen', the exile calls for wings to fly through life as in his youth, wings to fly to his homeland. Often he dreams he is borne aloft to starry heights, but the sun's heat melts his wings like those of Icarus and he plunges into the sea to be overwhelmed by the storms of life. There are fine moments: soaring arpeggios for the winged flight, syncopated chords, and a change of key all help to keep the interest alive in this long song. No. 9, 'Rose, Meer und Sonne', is a warm love-song; like many written with Clara at his side it has a very long postlude. This is quite an effective song, though the pianist has the best of it. No. 10, 'O

Sonn', o Meer, o Rose', takes up the theme of the previous song, but being in strophic form there are some awkward word settings in places.

A Heine trilogy, *Tragödie*, originally for chorus and orchestra, may have been written during the year though it was published as Op. 64, no. 3. It is a vigorous invitation from a lover to his beloved to fly with him. The piano has syncopated chords and the interludes have a right-hand melody decorated with turns, which incline one to believe that the song is quite an early work. A plaintive note creeps in when the man tells the girl that he will die if she does not come with him, however the postlude indicates that she does come, in a series of rising chords which suddenly drop, giving a chill feeling of disaster to come. The second song was said by Heine to be a folk-song and Schumann has set it very simply and with great economy. It has a short introduction in E minor. The narrator tells of a great frost in the spring night when all the flowers have withered. A man and a maid have fled from home, they have wandered hither and thither and in the end have died. This is most beautifully and touchingly set with the minimum of accompaniment. It leads into the third song which, unaccountably, Schumann has set as a duet, thus ruling out any likelihood of the trilogy being performed.

Also undated is a little 'Soldatenlied' by Hoffmann von Fallersleben without opus number. It is a child's quite delightful idea of being a soldier, set in a fine marching rhythm to a rousing tune. A not very inspired setting of 'Auf dem Rhein' by Immermann and a 'Liebeslied' by Goethe complete Op. 51, the other songs from which have already been discussed. The latter poem comes from notes on the 'Westöstlicher Divan' where it is headed 'Codes'. Certainly the words are very disjointed, but it is suggested that Schumann used the poem as a private code between him and Clara. It makes a very attractive piece of music even if the words are obscure.

The Songs of 1849

The wonderful year of song-composition which began in February 1840 was now, in January 1841, at an end. The composer was happier than he had ever been and the sorrows of the romantic poets were for the time being losing some of their appeal. Also he was feeling the need to spread his wings. Orchestral and chamber works were claiming his attention. In 1844 the family moved to Dresden, and only an occasional song appeared between then and 1849. He tells us that he is writing in a new style and that he is composing not of necessity but for pleasure.

In 1847 there is 'Soldatenbraut', Op. 64, no. 1, to words by Mörike. It is set in a delightful march rhythm and surely must have been in Hugo Wolf's mind when he wrote 'Der Tambour'. Also associated with Hugo Wolf is Mörike's 'Das verlassene Mägdelein', and Schumann's setting has become sadly overshadowed by the well-loved version of the younger composer; yet it has its own merits. There is a letter in which Wolf says: 'On Saturday I wrote, without meaning to, a setting of "Das verlassene Mägdelein", already set to heavenly music by Schumann.' Unforgettable as Wolf's setting is, it cannot displace Schumann's much simpler, less dramatic one. His little servant girl is completely sunk in misery and weariness, even the sparks of the fire cannot rouse her, a sforzando chord on the piano is the only sign of them. She rouses a little at the memory of her dream, but whereas Wolf's girl has an outburst of passion at 'plötzlich da kommt es mir', Schumann's climax, if one can call it a climax, is on the lingering crotchet bar at 'geträumet habe'. Schumann knew only too well the depths of depression, and for sheer misery this song has few parallels. There are likenesses between the songs, notably the use of thirds which surely must have influenced Wolf.

The chronicler's job begins to be a sad one, for though there was a recrudescence of song-writing in 1849 the strain of the intervening years was beginning to show. The wonderful spontaneity of genius had gone. Though Schumann could still write beautiful songs they become rarer. Where other composers have gone from strength to strength Schumann shows a deterioration until he ceased writing altogether.

Work on his opera *Genoveva* had aroused an interest in dramatic subjects and he now wrote some works for mixed voices. The first of these was a *Spanisches Liederspiel* by Geibel for four voices and piano, Op. 74. Only the solos are discussed here. No. 1, 'Melancholie', is a florid, dramatic song in quite a new style, almost operatic in treatment, with wide intervals and bravura passages more consonant with despair than melancholy. It is an effective song for a good soprano. No. 2, 'Geständnis', is a tenor song with a wide-ranging vocal line and cadenza, also distinctly operatic in style both in the melody and in the piano which begins to have a slightly orchestral feel about it. A third song without opus number, attached as an appendix, is 'Der Kontrabandiste' with guitar accompaniment. It is in a very bombastic style with many florid passages not really suited to Schumann's genius, unless, as has been suggested, it is meant as a parody, in which case it could be made amusing.

Another work to words by Geibel was the *Spanische Liebeslieder* for the same combination as Op. 138. The soprano air 'Tief im Herzen' is sadly overshadowed by Wolf's much profounder setting. He could well be forgiven for thinking he could improve on this one. The tenor has no. 3, 'O wie lieblich ist das Mädchen', a return to the Schumann we love. It is an enchanting song with delightful interludes for the piano in the strophic setting. It should certainly be heard more often, especially if paired with the next, 'Weh, wie zornig ist das Mädchen', 'O how angry she is! She goes into the mountains with her flock, as pretty as a flower, as angry as the sea, o dear!' The composer does not take her anger very seriously. The opening acciaccaturas wittily suggest petulance, and there is a caressing little figure on the piano when she is with her flock. It is good to have Schumann in light and witty mood in these two songs. The song for contralto is 'Hoch, hoch sind die Berge'; the girl watches her beloved go off up the mountain although she beckoned him with all her five fingers. The flowing piano accompaniment suggests the streams' sound which is all the answer she gets. No. 5 is for tenor, a 'Romanze' with a guitar-like accompaniment of great delicacy and charm. The poet tells the river Ebro to ask his beloved if she ever thinks of him. There are four nearly identical verses only varying in the last. It is an attractive song.

In 1848 Schumann had had success with his *Album für die*

Jugend for piano; now he had the idea of producing a similar album of songs. In this year 1849 revolution came to Dresden, so the family moved to Maxen and later to Kreischa. Like all good romantics, Schumann sympathised with revolutionary ideas, but, unlike Wagner, was not prepared to fight for them. So he wrote a few marches, then settled down to his *Liederalbum für die Jugend,* Op. 79. As Clara remarked to her diary: 'It is extraordinary how the terrible events without have awakened his poetic feeling in so contrary a way. All the songs breathe the spirit of peace.'

The songs are arranged in order of difficulty, ending with 'Mignon' on the threshold of a more complex emotional life. There are twenty songs, beginning with four very short strophic pieces suitable for the very young and exquisitely written. Schumann was the father of five children so he knew what children liked. The first six poems are all by Hoffmann von Fallersleben. No. 5, 'Vom Schlaraffenland', has undertones of satire, but Schumann ignores them and treats the subject of a land of cakes and marzipan with its entrance barred by a mountain of plum jam purely as an innocent child's idea of heaven. No. 6, 'Sonntag', the first one to be through-composed, is very attractive with a good tune over a flowing accompaniment. Two 'Zigeunerliedchen' by Geibel follow. The first, the story of a gipsy lad, who enlisted as a soldier, took his earnest money and deserted. Now he must hang. But when they came for him he got his shot in first. This immoral little tale is material for a clever musical character sketch of the slippery youngster, told with great economy and skill. The postlude with its offbeat accents is very expressive. The second gipsy piece is a sad little song of a girl stolen from her home at night. In the fifth and sixth bars there is an echo of Schubert's 'Das Mädchen'. The next song is Uhland's 'Des Knaben Berglied', chiefly distinguished by its horn-calls and a jolly tune. From the folk-collection *Des Knaben Wunderhorn* comes no. 11, 'Käuzlein', a strophic song about a poor little owl, terrified by the great owl, who flies away to hear the birds sing, but is driven away by the children who think his cry is unlucky. An acciaccatura on the first chord suggests his shrill cry and he has apologetic little grace notes in his melody. An open-air song from Hoffmann von Fallersleben is 'Hinaus ins Freie'; then we come to one of the gems of the collection, no. 12, 'Der Sandmann'. The piano part is full of minute detail as the sandman comes into the children's room with his sack. Creeping semiquavers over pianissimo staccato chords in the left hand suggest the stealthy tread on soft-soled shoes; there is a drop of a tenth because the sack is so heavy it weighs him down; staccato syncopated chords are the grains of sand he drops into the children's eyes as they say their prayers, and again where he gingerly steps out of their room. In the postlude the first theme gradually dies away as he departs and the children fall asleep.

Another gem is the well-known 'Marienwürmchen', no. 14, which has found its way into collections for adults. Though strophically set, the music fits all verses in this adorable tale of the child and the ladybird. Neither 'Die Waise' of Hoffmann von Fallersleben nor Hans Andersen's 'Weihnachtlied' with chorus are of great interest, but no. 18, 'Die wandelnde Glocke', is great fun. It is a cautionary tale of the boy who would not go to church. We hear the bell tolling, but he manages to run away to the fields, not heeding his mother's warning that it would come and fetch him one day. But the boy thinks: 'It is up in the belfry so I am quite safe.' The bell stops and suddenly he sees it come lumbering through the field behind him; the piano imitates its lumbering gait. Terrified he races back to the church and now he never waits to be called. In the postlude the bell goes on tolling. No. 19, 'Frühlingsankunft', is again by Hoffmann von Fallersleben, a wistfully attractive little song. 'Kinderwacht', by an unknown poet, is a young child's song very simply set. Of more interest is no. 22, 'Des Sennen Abschied' from Schiller's *William Tell*. The piano has a few bars imitating the sound of the herdsman's bag-pipes with the drone in the left hand persisting throughout the song. The herdsman leaves his summer pastures and promises to return when the cuckoo comes back and the streams flow again, in lovely May. There is a break at the repeat of 'im lieblichen Mai' after 'lieblichen' and the word is left in mid-air. Eric Sams suggests it is meant to indicate that the voice was carried off by the wind. No. 24, 'Er ist's' by Mörike, was later set by Hugo Wolf in a brilliant and exuberant manner. Schumann's setting is quite different; it is tender, and is directed to be sung *Innig* where Wolf's is *Sehr lebhaft jubelnd*. The prelude has a suppressed excitement and the 'fluttering blue ribbons of spring' are expressed in quick semiquavers in the voice part. A tender rising figure for the violets on the threshold of waking followed by harp-like chords usher in the sounds and arrival of spring. There are repetitions which build up the excitement of 'Ja, du bist's'. Surely this song has nothing to fear by comparison with the later one of Wolf?

No. 26, 'Des Buben Schützenlied', also from Schiller's *Tell,* is interesting for a note in the margin that it was 'composed on 3 May – Revolution in Dresden!' It has slight political under-currents which do not obtrude and were probably ignored by the composer. No. 27, 'Schneeglöckchen', is an exquisite miniature by Rückert. Flowers were always an attraction for Schumann and this is no exception. A delicate figure on the piano suggests the drooping heads of the snowdrops and also the little bells of the flowers which chime. Yesterday's snow has made them ring: 'What does their ringing mean? O come quickly for spring is here'. This is one of his most charming flower pictures which should be heard more often. There remain two songs by Goethe. 'Lied Lynceus des Türmers', from *Faust,* a song of the watchman, looking out from his tower. Somehow this poem did not inspire much response; the tune is rather matter-of-fact and lacking in variety. 'Mignon' is 'Kennst du das Land?' and will be left for discussion with the other *Wilhelm Meister* songs of Op. 98A.

After the collapse of the revolution, the Schumanns returned to Dresden, where Robert was busy working on a variety of com-positions, among them a *Minnespiel* from Rückert's *Liebesfrühling,* Op. 101. The first solo is for tenor, 'Meine Töne still und heiter', which is really two poems set as one. It is quite attractive though rather long. No. 2 is for soprano, 'Liebster, deine Worte stehlen', a warm and passionate love-song. It begins on the same chord as that with which the previous song had ended, with the first three bars in recitative; then the voice is off to an enthusiastic melody of thanks to the beloved, whose songs have so thrilled her. It is a good song for a woman's voice, though one must admit that it does have a few awkward angles in the melody. After this a lovely song for tenor, 'Mein schöner Stern', which has a personal appeal that is apt to be missing from some of the later songs. 'My lovely star, let not your brightness be dimmed by the mist in me. Do not drop to earth and me, rather raise me to your height.' The next song is for alto: 'O Freund, mein Schirm, mein Schütz'. It suffers from two handicaps, one, the text which bristles with consonants, the other, the original form of accompaniment:

Ex. 10

Putz! mein Stolz, mein Trost, mein Trutz! mein Boll - werk,

This very interesting figure throughout a whole song inevitably gets wearisome after two pages in slow tempo.

1849 was the centenary of Goethe's birth, a suitable moment for the setting of nine songs from *Wilhelm Meister*, a project Schumann had long had in mind. One cannot help wishing he had composed them earlier in his career, because the mental trouble from which he suffered periodically was not very helpful, or perhaps too helpful in setting such songs as the Harper's in which he got too much involved.

To take Mignon's songs first: 'Mignon', Op. 79, no. 28 and 98A, no. 1 – which are identical – is probably the most successful. For some reason, although he had a profound reverence for Goethe, Schumann was never at home in his verse as he was in Heine's or that of any of the younger poets. His setting of 'Kennst du das Land?' begins with a short prelude, then the voice enters to guitar or harp chords as Mignon describes the land where lemons and laurels grow. A little falling phrase suggests the familiar trees. Repeated chords represent the soft winds that blew; they then increase in intensity and fullness at 'Dahin' as her agitation mounts, then subside at her pathetic cry 'There would I go with thee'. The song is strophic in form and though the first two verses match well enough, the dramatic third verse suffers. No note is taken of the dramatic possibilities of the 'Drachen alte Brut' and 'die Flut' as in Wolf's magnificent setting. But the song is quite as successful as any of the other composers' settings, with the exception of Wolf's. On the other hand, 'Nur wer die Sehnsucht kennt' falls far behind either Schubert's or Wolf's settings. It has a certain pathos but is marred by excessive repetition. 'Heiss mich nicht reden, heiss mich schweigen' suffers from the same defect. It starts off with Mignon's dramatic appeal to Wilhelm not to question her. The key changes as she tells him that in good time night must give way to day and even the harsh mountain does not grudge the earth water from her springs; the piano changes to a rocking motion at 'Others have a friendly breast on which to weep'. The setting now seems to falter and the composer has recourse to repetition of the words 'und nur ein Gott' which destroys the tension. So much of the song is quite lovely that the end is a disappointment. 'So lasst mich scheinen bis ich werde' is Mignon's last song when she begs to be left dressed as she is, as an angel, with a premonition of her early death. Too much, too young, she has suffered, let her remain ever young, she prays. Again a good beginning becomes disjointed; awkward leaps in the vocal line and some unfortunate word stresses disturb the atmosphere.

The Harper's songs begin with 'Ballade des Harfners'. This unwieldy text proved too much even for Schubert, who had recourse to frequent stretches of recitative, and it is not a success in Schumann's hands where it is much overloaded with shifting harmony. The other Harper songs show signs of Schumann's own disturbed mental state. They are lacking in coherence in places and tend to ramble. In 'Wer nie sein Brot mit Tränen ass' the vocal line is very disjointed and the piano part is punctuated by sudden harp flourishes which do not seem to help the sense and are rather disturbing. They occur again in a long postlude. 'Wer sich der Einsamkeit ergibt' suffers too from some awkward word-setting. There are some beautiful moments – for instance, when the harper likens the stealing in of pain 'like a lover' – but then Schumann loses himself at the climax of 'dann bin ich nicht allein' and the voice is left poised with nowhere to go. Much the most successful is 'An die Türen will ich schleichen' which is set with much greater simplicity and economy. Ex. 11 well expresses the old man's groping progress with dragging feet and tapping stick.

Ex. 11

The voice is for the most part kept in a narrow range, without the angular leaps of the other songs. It is really moving, which the more elaborate songs are not. The set is completed by Philine's song, 'Singet nicht in Trauertönen'. She is the flighty little actress in the theatrical troupe, whom Wilhelm found attractive. It is perhaps the most successful of the *Wilhelm Meister* songs. Here the composer has thrown off the gloom and madness of Goethe's great poetry and has relaxed into frivolous sanity. 'Night is the time for fun and dancing, love and nightingales. Day has its troubles but night brings pleasure.' The light staccato accompaniment is full of sparkle. After the quasi-orchestral treatment of the other songs it is a relief to have again a pianistic piece of writing.

At the end of the year 1849 Schumann wrote three songs to texts translated from Byron's *Hebrew Melodies* by Julius Körner, all for harp or piano accompaniment, Op. 95. No. 1 is 'Die Tochter Jephthas' which voices the noble sentiments of the girl whom her

51

father's vow has doomed to die, as a sacrifice to save her country. The voice has a wide-ranging melody, which becomes rather angular from the frequent intervals of sevenths and diminished thirds of which Schumann had already made use in the Goethe songs. The accompaniment is unsustained and, with its arpeggiando form, rather more suitable for the harp than the piano. There is a snatch of independent melody when the voice is silent. It is a fine song in its way and quite worthy of performance. More attractive is the second song, 'An den Mond', another poem also set by Hugo Wolf at the end of his career as 'Sonne der Schlummerlosen'. The bare arpeggiando chords with which the song begins have an atmosphere of chill and hopelessness. One can compare this with the opening phrase in 'Mignon' where the same chord appears in arpeggio form. At 'Ach, wie kalt' this song may not achieve quite that wonderful effect of cold that Wolf's does, because of Schumann's labouring the point by repetition, but it is a very beautiful and effective song in its own way. The third song, 'Dem Helden', is a tribute to the hero who has fallen in his country's cause. The words are heroic, but the music tends to be less heroic than bombastic. There is little nuance in its virtually strophic treatment. The arpeggios and flourishes would probably be more acceptable on the harp than the piano.

The Last Years: 1850-52

The year 1850 found Schumann engrossed in orchestral composition in which his subjective experience was expressed, rather than in song. The fine literary taste of earlier days gradually seems to deteriorate and we find him spending his energies on inferior poetry. His natural tendency to sentimentality, kept well under control in 1840, is allowed to override discipline. In late spring he was composing songs again: a set of three, Op. 83, by various poets. An impossible text by Julius Buddeus, 'Resignation', is the first, followed by an attractive one, 'Die Blume der Ergebung' by Rückert, with a good vocal line; it suffers rather from being broken up in the manner of 'Der Nussbaum' but without the continuity of vocal and piano melody so miraculously achieved in the earlier song. But it is certainly worthy of an occasional hearing. 'Der Einsiedler' well evokes an atmosphere of stillness, but in places the words are awkwardly set. The date of the Schiller ballad 'Der Handschuh', Op. 87, is uncertain and may well be earlier. It is a long dramatic story set with considerable variety and skill. The direction *Mit durchaus freiem Vortrag* gives the singer great scope for dramatic interpretation. To very stately music the king enters with his courtiers. At a signal from him the various wild cats enter the arena, lion, tiger, leopards, each with appropriate well-differentiated music, with much snarling and lashing of tails. Suddenly, from a fair hand, a glove drops from the balcony and lands between the lion and the tiger. There is a nice touch of fear here as the glove drops. With feline mockery the Lady Kunigund dares Sir Delorges, if he really loves her, to go and retrieve the glove. In recitative we hear the knight leap into the arena and 'mit keckem Finger' flick it from between the beasts. A picturesque little figure suggests the action. The key changes. All hold their breath in admiration of his daring. In a sensuous phrase the Lady Kunigund greets the hero tenderly, but to staccato chords he flings the glove in her face saying: 'I want no thanks from you', and promptly leaves her. This is a very effective song for a dramatic singer and one of Schumann's more successful ballads.

Reverting to his old practice of concentrating upon a single poet, Schumann now sets six poems by Wielfried von der Neun as Op. 89. The first song, 'Es stürmet am Abendhimmel', is considered by Eric Sams to be the first song to show the beginning of the principle of thematic change, later to be developed and perfected by Hugo Wolf. The poems are in rather exaggerated language which is not very wholesome for Schumann. The song is about a love-affair between a cloud and the sun. There are some quite effective storm effects but this is not really very convincing as a song. 'Heimliches Verschwinden' has a rather dreadful poem, but musically there is an attraction in the flowing arpeggiando accompaniment over a left-hand melody. 'Herbstlied' has a curious motif in the bass in descending notes:

Ex. 12

pp

possibly suggested by the fall of autumn. The vocal line is much broken up and the song cannot be said to be very successful. 'Abschied vom Walde' is much simpler in both text and music and therefore more attractive. The poet bids farewell to the forest and says that he will not exchange autumn for anything. This is a pleasant if not very distinguished song. 'Ins Freie' begins with a loud horn-call in chords with both hands. A bass tune and staccato chords accompany the poet's desire for the joys of freedom, which the winds carry away. Quite the best of this set is 'Röselein, Röselein'. It opens unaccompanied in A minor: 'Rosebud, must roses have thorns?' There follows a delightfully Chopinesque figure in A major, introducing the poet asleep. He dreams of thornless roses, but wakes, in A minor again, to find thorny roses all around him; the streamlet laughs and bids him stop dreaming, for roses must have thorns. The postlude continues the rippling theme to the end. Just before the key-change to A minor there is an allusion to bar 12 of 'Herbstlied'. Two more songs to von der Neun's texts are 'Gesungen' and 'Himmel und Erde', Op. 96, nos. 4 and 5. The latter song has distinct echoes of an earlier style in the reiterated chords on the piano and the turn in the voice part. There is even a fleeting reminder of 'Lied der Suleika', Op. 25, no. 9.

The other songs of Op. 96 are by various poets. No. 1, 'Nachtlied' by Goethe, is 'Über allen Gipfeln ist Ruh'', unforgettably set by Schubert. It is, in consequence, difficult to approach Schumann's setting with a completely open mind. Schumann's approach is more detached than Schubert's; we have the impression that he is observing rather than experiencing the stillness of the night. But if we can put our memory of the other song aside, we can appreciate a very beautiful composition of the poem. No. 2 is by an unknown poet, 'Schneeglöckchen', not to be confused with the infinitely superior Op. 79, no. 26. No. 3, 'Ihre Stimme', is by Platen. The poet sings of the beloved's voice which can magically reach him even from a distance and is difficult to forget. There is a warm vocal line over an arpeggiando piano part. Here again we catch an occasional echo of 'Lied der Suleika'.

'Mein Garten' by Hoffmann von Fallersleben may have been begun in 1840 and revised later. It is no. 2 of Op. 77. 'All the flowers for a lover's garland are growing in my garden, only the flower of happiness you will not find. Whether or not it grows here, where it blooms – dear heart, be satisfied if you have striven.' At 'ob sie heimisch ist' there is a direct quotation of a phrase from Beethoven's *An die ferne Geliebte* which appears elsewhere in Schumann, for instance in the piano *Fantasie,* Op. 17, and the finale of the C major Symphony. There is a charm in this little song which recalls a happier period of composition. No. 3, 'Geisternähe', is by Friedrich Halm, who suffered the loss of the woman he loved by her marriage to another man. In the song the poet feels the comforting presence of the beloved in the breeze that blows upon his face. The delicate piano part is very descriptive and there is a spontaneity that has become increasingly rare in these later songs. No. 4, 'Stiller Vorwurf' (poet unknown), is a very sparse and chromatic little song of considerable poignancy. Last of Op. 77 is 'Aufträge' by L'Egru, a song beloved of high sopranos. Over a scintillating accompaniment of demisemiquavers the voice has a breathless vocal line and we imagine the lover running vainly to catch up, but never getting near his messengers. Here we have a taste of the old Schumann again.

Another attractive song is 'Die Meerfee' by Julius Buddeus, Op. 125, no. 3. Bright silver bells and soft maiden voices are heard as the sea fairy arrives in her pearly coach. A delicate staccato prelude followed by a delicious tinkle of the silver bells accompany the light staccato melody in the voice. The rise and fall of the vocal line add to the suggestion of the waves' motion as the fairy arrives. A lad in a boat watches the apparition in a half-dream; then it all vanishes into mist and the postlude carries the scene out of sight and sound. No. 5 is a 'Husarenabzug' by Candidus, a long and silly poem about a hussar's departure. Its arch humour is too much for Schumann and results in too many bugle calls, drum rolls, and bombast. No. 1, 'Frühlingslied' by Ferdinand Braun, is set to a charming tune, but five strophic verses are too many to sustain the interest. No. 2, 'Frühlingslust', is from Paul Heyse's *Jungbrunnen*. An attractive poem has evoked a delightful response. 'The roses are in bloom, how can one escape love? My path is in the woods and my songs fly up to the hill-tops.' The setting is very light and gay and there is a nice lift in the voice part at 'fliegen bis in die Wipfel hinauf'. The song is quite short and ideal for an encore.

In 'Mein altes Ross' by Moritz von Strachwitz, Op. 127, no. 4, a horseman speaks to his old horse, lamenting that their adventures are over. The song opens with a martial figure which in various forms dominates the piano part. The horse shakes his mane and whinnies, as his master reminds him of old times. A softening of the mood comes with a reminder of the old castle, where a white hand would caress him. But now all is gone and covered with snow. The postlude resembles a funeral march. A good song with many picturesque features.

Six poems by Nikolaus Lenau were composed as Op. 90, which begins with 'Lied eines Schmiedes' in strophic form. The smith's hammer strokes are well marked on the piano and the voice part is in folk-song style but of no great interest. Brahms was more successful with his smith's song. No. 2, 'Meine Rose', is lovely. The poet likens his beloved to a rose, drooping for want of water. He brings a cup and there is a rise in the vocal line as he raises it, with a sudden change from B flat major to G flat major for the drooping flower as it revives. He wishes he could pour out his soul for the beloved and revive her like the rose. The whole atmosphere is unusually sultry for Schumann. No. 3, 'Kommen und Scheiden', is nearly a very moving song, but it gets so involved in chromaticism and an overlong postlude that it does not quite come off. No. 4 is 'Die Sennin'. We had her counterpart, the herdsman, in 'Des Sennen Abschied', Op. 79, no. 22. Instead of bagpipes we now have a triplet semiquaver figure which continues for most of the song, with a suggestion of cowbells and even of a gentle yodel. The mountains echo the girl's song and have the quaint idea that if death or marriage takes her away the soul of the hills will remember her song. 'Einsamkeit' is marred by the obsessive use of a descending quaver figure throughout three whole pages. 'Der schwere Abend' in E flat minor is weighed down by death and gloom. As a study in depression it has a certain beauty.

Under the impression that Lenau, who had spent the last few years in an asylum, was dead, Schumann set a translation of an old Latin requiem, attributed to Abelard's Héloïse, as a tribute to him; it is appended to Op. 90. As it happened the poet was not yet dead, though he died soon afterwards. 'Requiem', with a piano part to be played 'wie Harfenton', has a beautiful vocal melody and a sense of reverence in the accompaniment. It is a little long, owing to Schumann's habit of repeating what has gone before.

At the end of 1850 the Schumanns moved to Düsseldorf where Robert had been offered a conductorship. For a while his health improved and after a lapse of some months he began writing songs again. At the beginning of 1851 he set two poems by Titus Ulrich, Op. 107, nos. 1 and 2. 'Herzeleid' is a sad little song of a hapless maiden looking down into the water; she lets fall a wreath of immortelles and the waves softly whisper 'Ophelia'. It is very sentimental but not without a wan charm. More interesting is the second one, 'Die Fensterscheibe'. A girl is cleaning her window and sees her lover ride by. A little figure on the piano describes his 'head in air' manner. With the shock of seeing him she puts her hand through the window-pane so that the blood runs over her hand. Another little figure shows us that the man has looked up at the sound of breaking glass. For the first time for so long she looks into his eyes. But he never looked when it was her heart that broke. Although Schumann makes little of the drama, the song is effective and touching. No. 3 is 'Der Gärtner' by Mörike, later to be set so delightfully by Hugo Wolf. There are strong resemblances and Wolf obviously knew Schumann's version. The music has much charm, but there are some unfortunate word stresses which detract from it. In no. 6, 'Abendlied' by Gottfried Kinkel, gently swaying crotchet triplets establish a tranquil atmosphere over which the voice sings in 4/4 against the 6/8 of the piano. It sweeps up a sixth at 'Wirf ab', cast away all care and fear. The song might with advantage have been a little less chromatic but it is very pleasing in its serenity.

Vier Husarenlieder, Op. 117, are effective manly songs by Lenau, written for a baritone. In 'Der Husar, trara!' the hussar is in boastful mood with many bugle calls and traras; in 'Der leidige Frieden' he laments, to a martial rhythm, the dullness of peacetime when his sword is rusting on the wall. 'Den grünen Zeigern' finds him in merry mood, singing with great verve; and finally, to a riding figure, 'Da liegt der Feinde gestreckte Schaar', he rides out to battle, returning in triumph with bloody sword to trumpet calls and rolling drums. These poems were a strange choice for so peaceful a composer but they are quite successful and a useful addition to the baritone's repertoire.

In contrast the next songs are all by a seventeen-year-old girl, Elisabeth Kulmann, whose early death had greatly moved Schumann, and, it must be feared, blinded him to the excessive naïveté of the poems and their unsuitability for serious composition. This Op. 104 consists of seven songs. Though Schumann cannot help writing some attractive music, he was careless about his word setting in several of them. The best are no. 3, 'Du nennst mich armes Mädchen', which has quite an attractive poem, and no. 4, 'Der Zeisig' ('The Songbird'), a frankly childish poem, set in a simple style. It is light, delicate and short, and it could well have had a place in the *Album for the Young,* Op. 79.

Other songs of 1851 include 'Die Spinnerin', Op. 107, no. 4, by Paul Heyse, the poem which, with some alterations, Brahms used in his Op. 107, no. 5. Unlike Brahms, Schumann imitates the spinning-wheel throughout the song, except where the girl wails that no one comes to woo her. Her hands falter for a moment and the wheel is still. It is not a great song but touching. No. 5, 'Im Wald', is by Wolfgang Müller. The poet, walking in the woods, sees the butterflies, birds and deer, all in pairs and sadly contrasts his own lonely state. The piano has a pleasant walking rhythm and a little rising arpeggio which perhaps suggests the butterflies' and birds' flight but is not suitable for the third verse when it precedes the deer. The song has a plaintive charm though it lacks distinction.

Three songs from Pfarrius's *Waldlieder* form Op. 119. 'Die Hütte' is in folk-song style to a jolly tune, but the composer's care in setting words has sadly deteriorated and, especially in strophic song, falls from the wonderful standard set by his early songs. 'Warnung' is a strange song warning the bird to be silent, because its song attracts the owl which will kill it. The piano has a curious figure repeated at intervals and some odd discords with the voice. The best of the set is 'Der Bräutigam und die Birke' which tells of a young man asking a birch tree what wedding-present it will give him. The tree offers a whole series of gifts which the man accepts but still asks for more. A charming little figure accompanies the tree's answers. Finally the tree says: 'I have given you all I have, I have only my bare life.' 'Then,' replies the young man, 'you live in hardship, so come with me and warm our room.' This delightful poem is set with much spirit and humour.

Only one more collection of songs was to come from the master. He composed, at the end of 1852, five texts translated by Gisbert von Vincke from the songs attributed to Mary Queen of Scots, Op. 135. The flame was now dying down and we miss a sense of inspiration in these not very promising poems. 'Abschied von Frankreich' has a flowing figure representing the Queen's lute. 'Farewell dear land where I have been happy. The boat bears me away from happiness.' There is an echo of the chords of 'An den Mond', Op. 95, no. 2, at 'Glück so weit'. 'Nach Geburt meines Sohnes', a prayer for her infant son, is rather awkwardly set to the vocal line over sustained chords on the piano. 'An die Königin Elisabeth' starts with a dotted phrase:

Ex. 13

which sets the tone for the direction *Leidenschaftlich*. It recurs in various forms throughout the song. The words of the poem are unwieldy and difficult for musical setting, as Schumann finds. The music, like the words, is restless and disjointed. The very touching words of 'Abschied von der Welt' have inspired a less complex setting, but it is difficult to keep up one's interest to the end. More successful is 'Gebet'. There is real urgency in the pleas that rise in pitch at each repetition; metre and rhyme are well matched. This is a real heart-cry from the suffering woman and the song is very moving. Op. 135 will always have a certain appeal on account of Mary Stuart's romantic character, but in their German dress the poems lose much of the appeal of the original texts.

These were Schumann's last songs. Early in 1854 his condition was such that he asked to be put in an asylum, after an attempted suicide by drowning in the Rhine, the river he loved so much and which drew such endearing music from him. There he died peacefully on 29 July 1856.

Summary

Where does Schumann stand as a song-writer? Historically, between Schubert and Hugo Wolf. He is the link between the glorious spontaneity of Schubert, who could, if so inclined, have set a time-table to glorious music, and the punctilious, literary and psychological Hugo Wolf. Schubert, though a romantic, still had a strong feeling for the classical age, among the older poets, for Goethe and Schiller. Schumann was a mystic and a musical representative of the nineteenth-century German romantic movement of Heine, Eichendorff and their fellows.

As a pianist, it was natural that he should give the piano an important role. At first his songs tended to be piano pieces with a vocal line added, often doubling the piano throughout, but in his best songs the piano acts as partner and commentary. Schubert first raised the status of the accompanist to partnership in his best songs, Schumann carried on a step further until perfect unity was achieved by Hugo Wolf. His influence on Wolf can be traced in songs like 'Das verlassene Mägdelein', 'Der Gärtner' and others and we know that he was much reverenced by Wolf.

He extended the harmonic freedom begun by Schubert. We know that he was considered very 'modern' by the Leipzigers. Even the adoring Clara sometimes begged him to compose something easier to understand. Typical were his leaps from key to key and modulation by enharmonic change; a fondness for chords of the dominant and diminished sevenths and his use of syncopation. In 'Intermezzo', Op. 39, no. 2, for instance, there is hardly a single note on the beat in the piano part throughout the entire song. He revelled in picturesque description: the stealthy tread of the Sandman in Op. 79, no. 12; the sound of drums and bugle calls, horns and horses' hoofs, guitars and silver bells. His gift for making the piano sound like an organ is manifest in 'Stirb', Lieb und Freud', 'Die Nonne' and 'Sonntags am Rhein'. Extreme despair called forth chromatic writing as in 'Nun hast du mir', the last of the *Frauenliebe und -leben* songs, and many others.

Something new he brought to music was his writing about night as something ominous or sinister, as in 'Zwielicht', Op. 39, no. 10, as opposed to its mysterious or magical aspect as in 'Mondnacht' or 'Schöne Fremde'.

He had an instinct for choosing poems which music could complete. For him music was inseparably bound up with his way of thinking. 'Everything that happens to me is expressed in music.' It is the first impression of a poem which impresses him; he often ignores such subtle implications as there may be in the poems. His friends were mostly liberal or radical in politics, but he would ignore the political undercurrents in poems like the *William Tell* ones in Op. 79 or Uhland's 'Des Knaben Berglied' and simply take them at face value. He has been accused of missing the irony of Heine in *Dichterliebe*, but is it not possible that he saw deeper into the real feelings behind the irony? We know that Heine fought hard against his romanticism and used *Stimmungsbrechung*, the negation or ridiculing of the mood produced by a romantic poem, as an escape from the dream world in which he lived.

Schumann chose texts largely and most successfully from those of his friends and contemporaries. But deeply as he loved poetry, he considered it inferior to music, so if occasion required it, he would not scruple to alter words or ignore the metre of the original, nor hesitate to fill out his musical requirements by repetitions. In his best songs, especially those by Heine, he would respect the text and say what further he had to express in the postludes. In his best songs he showed a fine sense of word values, in advance of any composer before him. It is one of the sad things about the later years that this quality deteriorated so seriously.

He was not at his best in folk-song style where his tunes were apt to be somewhat square-cut; nor in narrative songs where his dramatic sense was apt to falter, except in a song like 'Die beiden Grenadiere' in which his own emotions were stirred, owing to his admiration for Napoleon. He was apt to get bogged down in a long story.

His genius was shown in his power of catching a mood and clothing it with understanding and economy. He was essentially a miniaturist. A man of extremes of mood himself, he could enter into the emotions of his poets with fine psychological insight. On the other hand his too close involvement with the emotions of Goethe's Harper, at a time when his own mind was disturbed, may account for his comparative failure in the *Wilhelm Meister* songs. One feels that had he tackled this group in the days of 1840 the result might have been very different.

That he let his heart influence his judgement is apparent in some of the poems he chose, especially in the case of Elisabeth Kulmann, but even there he is saved from banality by his complete sincerity and his sympathy with her child mind. This also made his children's songs easily acceptable. That his taste and judgement deteriorated is evident in his choice of the exaggerated style of Wielfried von der Neun and unsuitable texts like those of the Mary Stuart songs.

His own nature had a strong feminine streak and his understanding of, and sympathy with, the feminine mind is unequalled even by Hugo Wolf, whose women tend to be rather unpleasant. Schumann's girls and women are treated with deep tenderness. Besides the great cycle of *Frauenliebe und -leben* are many other vivid pictures – the nun in 'Die Nonne' and the girl in 'Stirb', Lieb und Freud', the silly girl in 'Die Kartenlegerin', the charming and the angry girls in the Spanish songs of Geibel are only a few examples from the many.

Schumann has suffered from the anti-romanticism of the last few years and, with the exception of the three great cycles, the bulk of his songs have been rather neglected. People have a tendency to stop at Volume I of the collected songs with an occasional dip into Volume II, but Volume III also contains songs worthy of an occasional appearance in programmes. The last sad years caused a terrible falling-off of his powers, but he was still Schumann and even second-class Schumann has much to offer and delight us.

Of his place among the immortals there can be no doubt. It could be assured by a mere twenty or so of his songs alone, and he wrote far more masterpieces than those.

Index of songs and poets